CAPE FLATS

Love Affair

Stanley Jacobs

CAPE FLATS – Love Affair

Published by Tshienda Publications ® 2020,
South Africa
Copyright © 2020 by Stanley Jacobs All
rights reserved.
No part of this book may be reproduced or transmitted in any form or by any means, electronic or mechanical, Including photocopying, recording, or by any information storage retrieval system, without permission in writing from the author.

Design and lay-out by Haroldene Tshienda

ISBN: 978-0-620-87230-0

Revised version
Edited by: Olivia M Coetzee

(1st Edition, 2nd Print)

TABLE OF CONTENT

Foreword 5
Introduction 6

CHAPTER 1: Mandy 9
CHAPTER 2: Charlie & Janine 17
CHAPTER 3: The Meeting 22
CHAPTER 4: The Morning After 27
CHAPTER 5: The Unexpected 34
CHAPTER 6: New Beginnings 39
CHAPTER 7: Cape Point 45
CHAPTER 8: Valentine's Day 49
CHAPTER 9: Tony Cupido 58
CHAPTER 10: The Aftermath 62
CHAPTER 11: Moving In 65
CHAPTER 12: The Divorce 69
CHAPTER 13: The Wedding 73
CHAPTER 14: The Wedding Reception 78
CHAPTER 15: Deon Abrahams 83
CHAPTER 16: Charlie's Daughters 87
CHAPTER 17: Muizenberg 92
CHAPTER 18: Forgiveness 96
CHAPTER 19: Inheritance 103
CHAPTER 20: The Letter 107
CHAPTER 21: Family Matters 111
CHAPTER 22: The Funeral 117
CHAPTER 23: Counting Your Blessings 121
About the author: 127

The change starts within your mind. Be the change you want to see in your community.

FOREWORD

The Cape Flats is not just a place, it is a feeling. You literally have to eat, walk and have endless conversations with the people in order to understand the Cape Culture. It is a rich an authentic culture with a deep history. We present to you this amazing book, CAPE FLATS – Love Affair written by a remarkable, talented and passionate man, Stanley Jacobs.

The author takes us on a journey of self-discovery but at the same time, He is portraying the lifestyle of some couples and the challenges that they have to face daily to overcome poverty, rejection, pain and forgiveness. The consequences of one's actions and that love can conquer many things. This book is not a book for those who are looking for proper English or Afrikaans literature. It is the language that the Colored folks speak.

You will experience a different style of writing, yet it is packed with humour and emotions. I truly salute Stanley for sharing His talents with us and I hope you as the reader, will enjoy it just as much as I have enjoyed it. The love in relationships, the importance of family and the metaphor of oneness, is what Stanley is sharing and writing about. One thing for certain, is struggles does not last forever. Whatever you put your mind to, you can achieve it with dedication, consistency, and hard work.

Haroldene Tshienda – Writer & Publisher

INTRODUCTION

I dedicate this book to my late grandmother, Aunty Maraai from Gerard's Way. Life has not always been easy on her, but she was the best grandmother I could have asked for. Removed from her home in Constantia, a single parent, raising five children on her own. She could not read nor write but made sure her children and grandchildren went to school and encouraged us to better ourselves.

She passed away on 11 September 2005, it was the saddest day in my life. I told her, "Ek gaan vir Mammie Hermanus toe vat." I bought my first car much later only and unfortunately I never had the opportunity to fulfil that dream. I felt very sad when she laid in hospital and I could not do anything to help. I was standing next to her wishing, that I could just win the Lotto to put her in a Private Hospital to receive the proper care that she deserved.

My childhood memories are very special with her. When everyone gave up on me, she never did and always told me, "Stannie jy moettie worry nie, alles gaan oright wies." She had a way of hiding all her heartaches and disappointments behind her beautiful smile. I have dedicated my life to change lives on the Cape Flats because of her. I realised that this is my passion because there is more moms and grandmothers like her out there. One of the most important things she taught me was to never walk around with hatred in my heart. It took me years to master it. I learned that the past belongs in the past and if you do not deal with it on the spot, it will follow you everywhere you go.

The Cape Flats was birthed out of hatred, but it is my place where I was born and raised. I am indeed a proud Cape Flats Citizen. The people on the Cape Flats are unique and amazing. Do not get me wrong, we have a few that I do not want to be associated with. So much was taken from #mymense but we fought hard and we still do.

I can proudly confirm that doctors, lawyers, teachers, dentists, and maybe other high profilers were born on the Cape Flats. This is an indication that we have many hidden treasures out there. In some cases, we just need to nurture these raw diamonds as they go through the process of evolving into the gem they are supposed to be.

A plant cannot grow without water and the same goes for our children on the Cape Flats. We need to encourage them, and parents need to know that their presence are fundamental.

In conclusion, we can only make the Cape Flats a better place if we unite. Fight for what is right and bring that culture of, "I CAN" back to the Cape Flats. Change is needed and we need to be the change. It does not cost us a cent to be nice and to encourage someone and that is how we water our people. Our children need us, our communities need us, and it is time to get up and start working. We need to stop killing our own people and love our people, boast about our people. I am proud to be a Cape Flats Citizen and so should You. The Cape Flats taught me that they can steal whatever they want materially but they can never steal my spirit, it belongs to me.

#jouuncle

CHAPTER 1

Mandy

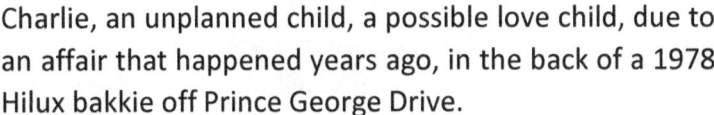

Charlie, an unplanned child, a possible love child, due to an affair that happened years ago, in the back of a 1978 Hilux bakkie off Prince George Drive.

Charlie's Mom, Aunty Mandy was at the Grassy Park Hotel. It was their school reunion and she went with a few friends to reminisce about the school bench memories. She was married to Anton and he could unfortunately not make it, to join her. She took a taxi from Ottery and met up with the few old school friends. Deon was also there, and the two had a history and still had hidden feelings.

During the evening, 'The Stylistics' cassette was entertaining the crowd.

Deon smaaking a blues, asked Mandy if she would dance with him. She wasn't very comfortable with the question, as she knew her husband was a very jealous person and did not want to stir any troubles, even though he was not there.

Deon insisted and she felt like he had put her on the spot and obliged to his request. As they swayed to the rhythm of the song, "You are everything" playing in the

background, the two of them started reminiscing about the old days as their bodies intertwined.
There is an intense passion amongst these two ex-lovers, as Mandy can feel the outline of a "cucumber" every time he draws her closer.

Mandy stops the dance to avoid him and returns to sit with her other friends. The evening is still young, and conversations are full of laughter and memories about the good old days at Grassy Park High.
Drinking, eating, and socializing with old friends was the order of the night.

Deon, who is already a divorcee, cannot keep his eyes off Mandy, she looks more attractive than before. Life must be treating her good, he thinks.

As the night progresses, Mandy starts wondering where Anton is as he was supposed to fetch her but has not arrived yet. She starts to panic and decides to call home from the public phone outside the Grassy Park Hotel, but no answer. Deon notices the anxious look on Mandy's face and enquires if she is ok, she informs him of the current situation and states she needs a lift home, as it's now getting late. He offers a lift and with no choice, she accepts. Deon has other intentions but does not make it too obvious. The reunion party is over.
Mandy gets into the white Hilux bakkie and glances at Deon. She realizes that Deon also still looks very good. He

has aged gracefully. He asks her, "Mandy hoekom het ek en jy nooit getrou nie?"

Feeling very awkward, she replies, "Jy was nie seker wat jy wou hê nie." An intense silence fills the bakkie.
The drive to Ottery now turns into a detour via Princess Vlei, where the bakkie comes to a stop. The sound of Peaches and Herbs playing softly in the background. Mandy senses a moment of guilt, as she thinks of Anton. She tells Deon, "Dink jy nie ons moet liewers gaan nie?" He has a faraway look in his eyes and remains quiet for a few seconds. "Ons kan nou gaan, but ek wil net vir jou sê, ek's nog lief vir jou."

The conversation now becomes very intermit. Deon reminds her about their first kiss at school in the girl's toilet. She was laughing, "Toe vang Julie ons mos amper," she says. The stars and moon shining in the dark night, giving the Vlei a majestic look. Deon puts his hand on Mandy's thigh, "Nee Deon, los my bout uit," and he removes his hand slowly.

She actually enjoyed it, but thinking of her vows to Anton, she stops it. Deon has no plans of giving up. The thought of the mattress in the back of the bakkie on his mind. He pulls Mandy closer as he moves closer to her.

The fingertip gear lever now touching his back. Mandy not stopping him recall thoughts of all the afternoons when they "vryed" at Klip Cemetry. Deon slides his hands under Mandy's dress and removes her black bloomer. She feels his touch on her body.

He unbuttons his bell-bottom pants. The bakkie steams up quickly. The silver horse on the front of the bakkie's bonnet has now vanished but another stallion is running around on the front seat. Mandy asks Deon while he is galloping inside of her, "Is jy nog rerig lief vir my?" "Of course, is ekke," was his fast response. She is feeling his passion and for a brief moment, she realizes that Anton is not as romantic anymore. Deon's stallion reaches the finish line, with black and white checkered flags flashing through his mind while moaning, compliments Deon's victory.
The two cuddle for a bit forgetting about everything and everyone else. They fall asleep in the bakkie and are greeted by the sunrise.

Mandy panics and starts composing herself, "Deon jy moet my huistoe vat." Deon still sleepy, from his adventure, eventually starts the bakkie and hit the road to Ottery. Mandy reveals her address, "Ek bly in Kevin Road," not sure where it is, he allows Mandy to give the directions. The sound of her voice is so angelic to him.

They arrive at Kevin Road. Outside the house is a blue Triumph and a big guy standing next to it. It is Anton waiting for Mandy.
She gets out of the bakkie and tells Deon, "Jy moet nou ry," but being concerned, he still asks "Gat jy ok wies?" She looks directly into his eyes and walks away.

Anton, is angry, shouting, "Waar was jy jou tief?" Trying to remain calm and composed, she calmly speaks back to him, "Jy het vergiet van my." Anton angrily smacks her, "Jy's sleg, ek kan sien jy het daai jong opgekap!" The neighbours are now outside and witnessing this commotion. He hits her again that she falls to the ground. Nobody came to assist Mandy; she eventually makes her way into the two-bedroom flat. Anton is in close pursuit behind her and bangs the door shut behind them.

The neighbors all talking about how abusive his behavior is, but no one called the cops. Mandy, feeling all battered and bruised, could feel the sensation of a blue eye slowly making an appearance. She takes a bath and listens how Anton is performing in the kitchen. She realizes the depth of her actions. She made a mistake, but it's too late now the deed has been done and the fact that she was so irresponsible by not using protection, left her with a lot of guilt and questions, het sy miskien nie dalk nou a STD nie of is sy nie dalk swanger nie?

A few months has now passed since the incident and she has become the victim of random abuse. Anton now would beat her almost daily. She was also now three months late. Her female curse has abandoned her.

Deon just disappeared off the face of the earth and she now has to face the music alone. At six months, everyone could see she was pregnant, and Anton knew he was not the father and wanted nothing to do with her and the child. It was time for her to give birth, all alone but she was keeping this child.

She was admitted to Victoria Hospital where she gave birth to a healthy boy. She named him Charles, but she called him Charlie. Anton never liked him and always referred to him as a "hoerkind" and his mother as a "tief". This really broke Mandy's heart but she felt this was the price she had to pay for her infidelity and made peace with it.

When Charlie turned three years old, Mandy was pregnant, and this time Anton was the father. He could not resist Mandy. She would bath with an open door and her muscular body would be on display for Anton to see. The muscles were a sign of her hard work around the house and walking a lot.

There was now a fourth member in the house, his name was Reginald. His father called him Reggie. Anton made it clear that he will never treat Charlie as his son, he would not inherit anything from Anton. Mandy could not treat her sons as step kids. She loved both sons unconditionally and never compromised her relationship with them.

The nonsense started when they went to school, Charlie had to attend Stephen Road Primary school while his brother went to Sid G. Rule Primary. Mandy became very sick and was diagnosed with cancer.

She went for treatment but did not do too well. Her boys were now at high school. Anton was not much bothered about Mandy or Charlie. He even told his estranged wife to arrange with her family to look after Charlie, should she die.

He made sure she understood that what was happening to her is her payback for her infidelity and that Charlie will always be bad luck. Mandy remembers the night Charlie was conceived very well, she called Anton several times, but he never answered the phone, where was he? Why does he not fetch her?

Worried about her boys and what would happen to them when she passes away, Mandy lost the battle against cancer and Anton disowned Charlie. He went to live with Mandy's brother Trevor, he was the only one that agreed to look after Charlie.

Trevor had a gambling problem and was always in trouble with the gangsters in Lotus River. Charlie did not like where he was living but had no choice. Him and his brother Reggie lost contact, it was as if Anton did not want to see the boy.

Charlie had no choice but to endure it, no one wanted him and was now the black sheep in the family, although he did not do anything wrong. He was never invited to any of his family's weddings and parties. He would always hear about these parties afterwards and now that he was living with his Uncle Trevor, no one came to visit Trevor either.

Lotus River, where most youngsters turn to gangsterism as the only solution, Charlie decides to get him a hobby that would keep him busy and chose to play soccer. He joined a soccer club in Grassy Park and played soccer every weekend, it was his way to escape his problems. He made a promise to his mom that he won't turn to gangsterism and he will work hard and not become another statistic. Uncle Trevor was also never at home. Between his gambling and working, he seldom came home on weekends. Charlie had to sort of look after himself.

It was here, where he learned to hustle by offering gardening services in his community. He had a few customers and that helped him to pay for his soccer and purchase food when Uncle Trevor did not come home. It was his way of thinking that saved him and kept him going.

CHAPTER 2
Charlie and Janine

Park Avenue in Grassy Park was full, and the music was good. Young Charlie was dressed in a white jean with a pair of chocolate Grassies, oatmeal shirt and a sleeper in his ear.

Charlie went with his friend David to have a good time and also try out his "game skills" on the opposite sex. There was a group of girls that was enjoying themselves and very friendly. A young girl named, Janine was one of them and Charlie wanted to talk to this girl with the blue Levi jean, blue denim shirt and Doc Martens shoes.

David: "Charlie kô ons gat sê hello vir dai kinders?" Charlie: "Ja ek het hoekal my oë op een van hulle." The two went and introduced themselves, as Tevin Cambell's music played in the background. Janine has also been watching Charlie and welcomes his company into the group.

Charlie: "Hi girls, my naam is Charlie en die is my coupling David." The ladies greeted the two politely and Charlie did not waste time as he moves closer to Janine.

Charlie: "Wat's jou naam?" he asks.
Janine: "My naam is Janine, ek is vannie Cafda, Komolosie straat, wil jy my nommer oek hê?"
Charlie impressed and overwhelmed responds, "Wel jy mag dit maar gee, ons might as well die formalities uit die pad kry," with a Cape Flats ougatte laggie.
Janine: "Stadig nou outjie, koep my eers 'n drink en dan kry jy dit."

Charlie got the lady something to drink as he continues his charm with Janine. David his friend, also striked it lucky and is chatting with Janine's friend Sonja. The evening is still young, and the new friends enjoy the music and company of each other. The girls decide to leave at eleven thirty. Charlie and David, being two real gentlemen, accompany the ladies down 5th Avenue to their destination in Cafda.

Janine is very impressed by Charlie and gave him her number and told him to meet her next week at Wynberg Park. The week dragged forever as Charlie wanted to really meet up with Janine. He decides to call her the Wednesday night. Her father answers the phone, "Hello."

Charlie: "Hello Uncle, kan ek met Janine praat asseblief?" The father responded, "Ek issie jou uncle nie, hou aan," as he shouts," Janine hier isse jong oppie phone vir jou."

Janine: "Hello."

Charlie: "Hi Janine is Charlie, hoe gaan dit?"
Janine: "Hello jy, watte surprise."
Charlie: "Wie is dai uncle wat die phone opgetel het?"
Janine: "Is my pa, hy is 'n seeman."
Charlie: "Oh, ek sien, is ons nog aan vir Saterdag en hoelaat?"
Janine: "Ja ons is nog aan, ek sal 'n kombers bring vir ons..."
Charlie: "Great ek sal sien wat ek kan bring, sien jou Sarâg."

Before you knew it, it was Saturday and the two met at Wynberg Park. They got to know each other a bit more and there was not a lot of people around except the grandma and granddad next to them. Charlie enjoyed Janine's company. Janine was nineteen years old turning twenty, and Charlie was twenty-one.

Time passed by so quickly as the two were getting to know each other. When it came to 4:30pm most people were leaving but the two had no plans of leaving yet. After 5pm, it seemed as if everyone was gone and they were alone. Janine did not wait long, she moved for Charlie's lips forced her tongue and kissed him passionately. It was Charlie's first kiss. He tried to kiss his arm a few times because David told him it's the best way to practice.

Janine who was an old expert, strokes Charlie's chest hair as she kisses him. He enjoys the attention and immediately has a problem as his Goliath awakes from a deep sleep. Janine feels something poking her through Charlie's crinkle cut tracksuit. The afternoon turned out to be exciting as Janine greeted the giant with a handshake. Charlie immediately goes into a fit of pleasure not knowing what happened as his toes starts to curl.

The two decide to leave the park and head home from Wynberg to Cafda. Janine introduces Charlie to her Mom. Her father was not home but Aunty Loraine was impressed with the young man her daughter brought home. Charlie clicked very well in the family and started to sleep over on weekends.

Six months after the two met, Janine found out she was pregnant and the two had to get married before the family finds out. It was a small wedding and had to be done before Janine's stomach started to show. After living with Janine's parents for a year they got a flat in Parkwood. Janine also got a job at a local hospital and the opportunity to study nursing.

Baby number two was also on the way now and the couple was slowly outgrowing each other. The relationship has turned into basic chitchat of just hello and goodbyes, the words "I love you" were no longer being shared. Charlie wanted to be a good father.

It turned out that Janine had an admirer at work. He always complimented her on how she dressed, and Janine loved the attention.

Her admirer would also bring her gifts and even bought her flowers. The "sacred ring" was removed when Janine gets to work. The picture of Charlie and kids were also replaced by a picture of her only. Everything between Janine and Charlie became an argument and soon their children started to pick up and it affected them as well. They also stopped taking their children to the park on Saturdays.

The laughter in the house has ended and all you could hear was a couple fighting over simple things like close the door, why didn't you eat up all your food, is my food not good enough, etc.

CHAPTER 3
The Meeting

On his way to work as per daily routine, he takes a taxi from Parkwood to Wynberg, just like any other morning. He greets everyone as he gets into the taxi "Môre Aunty Sybil, môre sê Uncle Iekie." He makes his way to the second row of seats, where he always sits. He notices a new face in the taxi and greets "Mornings," not knowing how the new passenger would respond. She replies, "Môre."

The taxi guard, shouting from the front seat of the van, "Stuur maar die fare vorentoe." As they take the turn onto the M5, the new lady loses her balance and stumbles onto Charlie's lap, grabbing at his chest. Feeling very uncomfortable, she apologizes to him saying, "Sorry ek het dit nie gemean nie."

He nods his head and says, "It's ok," blushing and stuttering at the same time. Something happened between these two commuters, it was as if their souls connected.

Everyone is getting ready to get out of the taxi, as it arrives at Wynberg taxi rank. Still feeling embarrassed, she gets out and he follows her.
She stops and he accidentally bumps into her from behind. Very uncomfortable, he reacts and says, "Sorry." She makes a joke and says, "Is kicks nou," and both of them start laughing. The smell of Brut cologne lingering in the air.

Both making their way to the Mowbray taxi. Charlie then introduces himself as Charles, "But almal noem my Charlie." She introduces herself, "Ek is Samantha but almal noem my Sam," she giggles.

"Nice to meet you Sam." She replies, "Likewise Charlie." He asks her where she is from and she answers that she recently moved into a flat in Parkwood with her mommy and enquires about Charlie. He responds by saying he lives in Blackbird Avenue with his family. Failing to mention with his wife Janine and their two daughters.

The two continue their journey to Mowbray talking about this and that but very passionate about politics. As they approach their destination, they get out and greet each other. A few days has passed, it's 5pm and Charlie needs to catch a taxi to Wynberg. In the taxi sat the beautiful Sam, he greets her in a flirtatious manner, "Hello stranger." She answered, "Hi Charlie, ons bump weer in mekaar," both laughing, reminiscing about their last experience.

The taxi, driving towards Wynberg playing love songs, the taxi gaartjie compliments Sam and says, "Julle twee maak mos 'n mooi couple," thinking that the two of them are a married couple, as both are wearing rings. Sam just smiles and Charlie appears nonchalant, acting as if he never heard anything. Charlie asks Sam for her number and if he can add her on WhatsApp. They become travel buddies immediately, "The drive from Parkwood to Wynberg can become very creepy especially winter season," he mentions.

Having each other's WhatsApp numbers, the two now also start chatting and following each other's profile statuses. They are now becoming very comfortable with each other and Sam would bake biscuits and crunchies for Charlie very often.

Something was now sparking between them and both knew what was about to happen. Ignoring the signs, the two of them continued their friendship.

They have lost themselves to each other since the first day exchanging numbers. Charlie's wife Janine one day went through his phone asking him who Sam was. Charlie would delete the messages daily, but his wife saw the status update of a recent picture. He lied and said, "Een van die staff byrrie werk." his wife replied, "Sy is pragtig."

Sam's company was now working overtime, a big order had to be shipped to California. She had no choice but to work late. She tells Charlie about her situation and that she wasn't sure how she was going to get home. Charlie, overwhelmed by his feelings for her, comforts her by telling her not to worry, he will ask his friend Lester to assist.

∗∗∗∗∗∗∗∗∗∗∗

Wednesday night at 9pm, Charlie waited outside Sam's place of employment. Waiting for her in his friend's modified Golf Mk1 with a dropped suspension, 17" mags and a sound system that's playing Chaka Khan's song, "Through the fire" on repeat. Sam gets in the car and greets him "Naand Charlie, dankie dat jy my ko haal het." Charlie replies, "Isse pleasure Sam."

Driving from Mowbray to Parkwood, Charlie ask Sam, "Wil jy virre spin gaan?" She replies, "Ja sal lekker wies." The route now changes from Claremont to Hout Bay. The song selection also changes from Chaka Khan to Boyz II Men. Charlie not really knowing what he is doing stops and parks a few meters away from the 12 Apostles Hotel, watching the moon shining bright amongst the stars and its reflection playing like a 3D movie in the sea.

Sam told Charlie, "Dit is mooi en so rustig." Charlie replies, "Sam daai's hoe ek oor jou voel." Not knowing what to say Sam answers, "But Charlie jy's getroud my vriend." For a few minutes, there was an awkward silence. Charlie rejects the term "friend" in his head, he ropes Sam over and kisses her. She pushes him away and says, "Charlie ons kannie, jy's getroud." He stutters as he tries to convince Sam, "Maar eeekkkk isss Liiieeef viirrr jou." He kisses her again, and this time Sam starts to kiss Charlie back and says, "Die is verkeerd Charlie." The two are now engaging in something that is forbidden but yet so tempting.

Charlie puts his hands through her straight black hair, not wanting to rush he touches her thigh slowly, Sam removes his hand as she grasps for her breath, she whispers in Charlie's ear and says, "Charlie my man het my seer gemaak en ek wil nie jou vrou seer maak nie." The two stop and he decide that it's better if they end this episode and rather go home before things really get out of control.

The Golfie starts up and the two leave for Parkwood. The mood changes and the sounds of Tupac is blaring from the speakers. The free flow system tells that Charlie is now rushing to get home. He stops in front of Sam's home, "Sam ek is sorry."
She replies, "Is ok Charlie, ek sien jou môre oggend," and gets out of the golf.

CHAPTER 4

The Morning After

The following morning Charlie waits for Sam at the spot where they have been meeting for the last few months. A shy Charlie greets softly, "Môre Sam." Sam looks at Charlie and responds, "Môre Charlie, dankie vir die lift."

The two do not want to engage openly as other commuters are standing close by, and after the confrontation with Aunty Susan who already asked Charlie if he is jolling - having an affair with Sam, the two rather stare deep into each other's eyes.

The next few days passed with little conversation between Charlie and Sam, and the tension in the air is noticeable. Sam decides they need to talk and makes the first move. She sends Charlie a message saying, "My vriend wat gaan aan met jou?" Unfortunately, Charlie forgot to take his phone with him that evening as he took Chester, his pit bull for a walk. Janine responds to Sam from Charlie's phone, "Sorry but Charlie het vir Chester, sy hond, vir 'n walk gevat." Not knowing how to react to this response, she politely replies, "Ek praat môre met hom dankie."

Sam decides that it is in the best interest that she and Charlie end their friendship. She will not be kept liable for breaking up a family. The next day, as they exit the Wynberg taxi, Sam calls Charlie one side and address him. "Charlie, ek het oor ons situasie gedink, en ons kan nie meer vriende wees nie." Charlie, taken aback by Sam's words, not sure how to respond, but slowly he mutters, "Sam is jy seker die is wat jy wil hê?" Sam, feeling fragile answers, "Ja Charlie," and walks away with tears streaming down her cheeks.

Months has now past, Charlie still reminiscing about what could have happened if he was not in such a hurry. Maybe they could have still been friends. Sam just disappeared, as if she never existed. Her seat in the van is now filled by a new Aunty Evelyn who loves to gossip. The smile and laughter that once lit up the vibe in the taxi, is now no longer. The taxi drive to Wynberg has lost its spark. The pleasure of driving in the taxi is all gone.

One morning, Uncle Iekie reached over to Charlie asking him, "Waar is daai mooi goose dan?" Charlie not knowing how to respond, says, "Sy wêk 'n ander shift Uncle Iekie." Uncle Iekie responds, "Ons moet maar oek daai shift werk," with a Cape Flats giggle. (Ougatte laggie).

Six months have now passed, and it is festive. By now, Charlie has made peace that he is no Romeo, fairy tales only happens in romantic books. Janine, his wife, who is a nurse, is now also working strange shifts. When Charlie comes home she leaves for work. The couple are now living past each other due to Janine's night shift duties and their daughters are with their grandparents for the holidays. Charlie alone at home, walks his pit bull Chester every night to escape his reality of feeling lonely.

American Clothing has a sale and Charlie gets ready to go buy his Christmas outfit, a green paisley shirt, cream trouser and a tan pair of Crockett & Jones. His Cuban hat he will purchase at Harrington's. As he makes his way from American Clothing he sees a familiar face. It is his Sam, she is walking in his direction, with her mother, Aunty Charlene. Sam notices Charlie as well. Feeling all flustered and shy, she stops and introduced her mother to Charlie, "Mammie die is my vrin, Charlie." Charlie's eyes are like magnets, starring only at Sam's beautiful full black eyes. Charlie only having eyes for Sam at this moment.

Finally, Charlie acknowledges the Aunty and greets, "Hello Aunty." Aunty Charlene picks up on the tension between Sam and Charlie, not wanting to make it obvious she greets Charlie, "Hello Charlie, nice om jou te meet." Sam changing the focus, "Charlie, ek sien jy't gaan shopping by jou favourite store."
He responds with a slight glimpse, "Ja 'n man moet mos daam reg lyk virrie big days." Aunty Charlene sensing that these two need to talk, excuses herself and tells Sam, "Ek gat jou by daai winkel kry." Sam replies, "Ek kom nou. Is reg mammie." Charlie full of excitement, mumbles, "Sam ek mis jou en jy lyk mooi in jou full

length wit rok." She stares at Charlie with gratitude, thinking no one really compliments her and makes her feel the way Charlie does.

Charlie also notices that she is wearing matching blue underwear, beneath the white dress. He wants to tell her that blue is his favourite colour, but he is lost in appreciation of admiration of her plus size body through the dress. Before the two could continue talking, Aunty Charlene comes out from the shop and tells Sam, "Ons moet nou gaan," and the three greet each other.

As the mother and daughter leave to take a taxi to Parkwood. Charlie cannot help to stare at Sam as she walks away. Her vision is beautiful, long black hair flowing like waves as she walks, the blue thong matching with the blue balconette bra. Slowly the two disappear and he decides he no longer need the Cuban hat. He decides to walk to Claremont, as he walks, he realises how much he loves Sam and he cannot live without her. He and his wife have now outgrown each other, and this happened before Sam even arrived on the scene. He and Janine got married very young, they were only 22 years old and wanted to escape reality.
He cannot remember when last he felt this way for another woman. The feeling is just different with Sam.

A few days later, Sam's mom approaches her, "Wie is Charlie nou rerig?" Sam, all shy and feeling guilty responding, "Ek gewag vir Mammie. Hy is getroud en ek is verlief op hom." Aunty Charlene, shocked, reacts and says, "But Sam, jy wiet wat met jou gebeur het." Sam keeps quiet and put on her headphones to escape the memories. She listens to some James Ingram. Her favourite song, "How do you keep the music playing" on repeat, she loves this big, handsome guy, but Charlie is not like any other man. He is funny, wise and even though he don't have a six pack anymore, he makes her feel important and loved.

Charlie sitting in his Apartheid-donated flat in Blackbird Avenue, pondering about his current situation and how this will end, is startled by Janine's constant complaining about living in Parkwood. Always nagging to Charlie about "Wat soorte man is jy wat so min pay, jy doen niks om jouself te beter nie, jy kan liewers study terwyl jy daai stupid hond loep." Lucky for him he has now managed to switch off when Janine starts her tantrums at him.

Driving his fiends Golf Mk1, he picks up Sam, takes a drive to Soetwater. The place is empty not a person in sight. He tells Sam about Janine and how she has been treating him. This brave man now shedding a tear
as he shares his inner feelings with Sam. He stutters as he opens up. Sam holds Charlie as he starts crying and comforts him "Charlie moettie huil nie, alles gaan ok wies."

Sam's soft, white complexion hand plays with his freshly cut fader. Charlie now resting his right hand on her left plus-size thigh, covered by a Levi denim dress.

The attention he is getting from Sam makes him feel so loved that his Lee jeans is looking for air as Sam unbuttons his jeans. He in return removes Sam's Levi belt. He unbuttons Sam's dress; he caresses her beautiful curved body. She asks him, "Charlie is jy lief vir my?" He replies, "Ek's baie lief vir jou."

It becomes intense as the two expressed their feelings towards each other in the abandoned Lighthouse at Soetwater, where many episodes like this one already played. As they reach Kilimanjaro simultaneously, he feels someone bumping their elbow into his ribs,
"Lê stil, jy maak sounds." his Woolworths pyjamas he got from a connection in Athlone, soaked with sweat,
he realises it was just a dream. Wide-awake after that abrupt awakening, he decides to get into the bath
in their one-bedroom apartment, but first he needs to boil water. The geyser will most probably be replaced one day but for now the Game-purchased Cauldron, should do the trick.

Sunday afternoon, Janine leaves Charlie to take care of the children, as it is her Sunday to work and she can't afford to be late. Charlie's estranged brother Reggie decides to visit him and the children.

Charlie offers his brother Reggie coffee and his brother shouts from the dining room, "Charlie ek drink mossie Riccofy nie." Standing with a pot of Jacobs in his hands, Charlie decides to shout back, "Dai is al wat ons hier drink Reggie." Already agitated Charlie ask his brother, "Wat

soek jy?" Reggie retorts "Ek wil jou net my nuwe kar wys." Shocked Charlie instantly changes his tune and ask his brother to take him and the girls for a spin.
Reggie decides to take the family for a surprise visit to Janine at work, the girls are very excited.

They arrive at the hospital and Charlie goes inside to call his wife. He sees a colleague and asks, "Waar is Janine?" The lady replies, "Sy was nou hier, sy is saam met Doctor in haar kantoor." Charlie heading to the office at the end of the long passage, he can hear a familiar voice. As he gets to the door he hears ruffled voices but can't hear what the conversation is all about. He knocks twice and then opens the door, only to catch his wife with the doctor, getting dressed. He immediately apologises and closes the door and wonders if he really saw what he saw.
His wife, Janine, comes out of the office and shouts at him, "Hoekom embarrass jy my soe?"

CHAPTER 5

The Unexpected

———————◦———————

Year after year Charlie has been told how useless he is and how he cannot think for himself. All this negativity takes him back to when he was thirteen years old. His father unemployed and very abusive towards Charlie and his mother, always hitting him for nothing and calling him degrading names. As far as he can recall, people have been using him as a punching bag. The manager he works for, also picking on him daily and some of his work colleagues always playing pranks on him. He realized, it is only with Sam that he feels like a man, loved, and appreciated.

As Janine enters, their once loved-filled home, where some very intense lovemaking sessions took place, she shouts, "Jy jou blerrie gemôs." Charlie now figured out what was happening and that his wife is now in love with another woman, doing some scissor cuts during working hours. Charlie retaliates and shouts back at Janine, "Jy kan 'n divorce kry, ons is klaar!" Janine who never lost a fight with Charlie, was not expecting him to retaliate. She suddenly feels like she was losing her rank as the woman of the house, picks up a dog ornament they received from a woman who collected clothes from them, a few years ago and threw it in Charlie's direction, catching his left shoulder. Janine screaming, "Charlie jy sal nooit bieterre as my kry nie." Charlie, thinking of his father who used to beat him and threw objects at him, gets up without saying anything, walks out the front door and head straight to Sam's house. He knocks on the door, and Aunty Charlene opens and says, "Hello Charlie," and he replies, "Hello Aunty Charlene, is Sam hier?"

Aunty Charlene not knowing what to say, thinking of what the neighbours would say when they see a married man visiting Sam, responds to Charlie "Ja maar jy kannie lank bly nie." He nods his head in agreement and Aunty Charlene calls out to Sam, "Charlie is hier vir jou!" Not expecting any visitors at that hour of the night, Sam comes out of the bedroom, just as Charlie turns around after closing the front door, sees Sam in a nighty, looking very comfortable without a bra. Her mother tells her, "Trek vir jou 'n gown aan."

Sam returns to the dining room after obeying her mom's request. Nervously, Sam asks him, "Wat maak jy hier die tyd vannie aand Charles?" Charlie feeling all flustered and full of emotions, starts stuttering as he cannot control himself, answers, "Is Janine."

Sam: "Wat van Janine?"
Charlie: "Sy jol met 'n ander vrou."

Sam thinking he was joking, "Praat djy weer nonsense?"

Charlie tells her what had happened and shows her his swollen shoulder from the ornament incident. Aunty Charlene, who is in the next room but listening to the conversation goes to the bathroom to return with lukewarm water with some Dettol added to it, telling Sam, "Maak dit skoon, Charlie moet nou gaan, julle wiet hoe die neighbours is," Aunty Charlene instructs.

Charlie leaves a few minutes later not sure about his next move. He needs to think about his future. He arrives home, takes his camping chair, headphones, and a blanket to sit with his best friend, Chester the dog. Tonight, he is not sharing a bed with Janine.

He listens to a Boyz II Men song, "End of the road", over and over. Thinking aloud, Charlie announces, "Ek's kla met Janine. Ek wil happy wies." With only Chester as his company, listening to his owner, not knowing what was happening, Chester jumps onto Charlie's lap and starts licking him as he can sense that Charlie is not himself.

The next day Charlie decides he needs to see a lawyer. There must be a cheap lawyer somewhere in Town. Janine on the other hand, calm as can be, is on the phone with her mother, "Mammie Charlie wil skei, hy wil my en die kinders lôs." Charlie's mind is made up, the only people he will look after are his two kids and Chester. He now finds himself a guest in the dining room of his own home. Sleeping on the floor with a mattress he took from his daughters' double bunk. Janine, no longer hiding her relationship, allows her lover to pick her up at the flat. Spending more time openly together and disappearing weekend after weekend. Sam is chatting with him more often now on WhatsApp, but still not ready to be seen with him in public, as people will judge them by assuming he left his family for her.

The day arrives, he is finally divorced and free from Janine. He is now renting a bungalow and Chester is living with him at his Aunty Rose's place in Dove Road, Parkwood. Sam is now more comfortable with the situation and is often visiting him at his new place. She decides it's time that Charlie and she spend a weekend together. Charlie books a chalet for them at Goudini Spa. It has been a rough few months for her Charlie and he needs to be pampered.

After the two spent the Friday night at the warm baths, enjoying each other's company, they make their way back to their chalet where a night of passion awaits these two lovers. Sam, always concerned about her appearance, tells Charlie, "Kyk hoe het my hare nou gemince," as her hair was wet and curly from the warm baths. Charlie replies, "Jy lyk sexy Sam. Charlie, feeling all aroused as he has waited for this moment since their first encounter in the taxi. Sam, sensing the moment, takes control and tells Charlie, "Ek's nou hier, hou jou reg big boy." Charlie responds, "Ek is al lankal reg," (met sy ougatte giggle).

Charlie is now playing some RnB jams and move over into the comfortable arms of Sam. He searches for Sam's full lips and outlines her lips with his tongue, gently opening her lips. He gently reaches for her hands, to feel her passionate touch. His lips now move from her lips to her neck. Inhaling her faint perfume smell, Issey Miyake, which she had purchased from Farieda at work for half price. Charlie compliments her, "Mmm, jy ryk lekker Sam." He touches her thigh exactly as he did in his dream. Sam giggles like a young lady, alive with passion. He moves his hands now to her lower back, brushing ever so slightly on her bum cheeks. Enjoying the feeling, he grips her bum cheeks, they feel like beautiful firm peaches. Even the stretch marks blend into the dermis of her skin. Everything about Sam is so heavenly. Sam, waiting to be in control and hungry for Charlie, as it has been years since someone has woken up her inner drive. She slowly straddles Charlie.

Charlie thinking that if the bed breaks, he will lose his deposit but never mind that deposit, this is what he has been waiting for. The passion is so intense, their heart rates are now above average, as they wrestle each to be on top and fight for the belt. This time Charlie reaches Kilimanjaro with Sam. As they explode in unison, all exhausted and gasping for breath, Sam asks Charlie, "Charlie is jy alright?" As he is breathing heavily.
He responds, "Ja ek is Sam, daai was lekker." Laying hand in hand next to each other, they now cuddle and eventually fall asleep. The seven minutes seemed like almost an hour of pleasure.

CHAPTER 6

New Beginnings

Sunday morning and the couple leaves Goudini Spa, heading for Parkwood, in a borrowed Golf Mk1. In love and feeling optimistic, Charlie pulls the car over, Sam concerned about the sudden stop, asks him "Wat is fout Charlie?" He leans over and takes out a black box with Galaxy Jewellers engraved on it. He looks straight into her eyes, and says, "Sam trou met my?" In sy mind dink hy, issie romantic om in a Golfie engage te raak nie but hy kannie waggie.

Dejavu! Instant flashes of their previous engagements flash in their minds. Not wanting to get hurt again but also aware that they cannot afford to lose out on each other. Sam blushes as her adrenaline level skyrockets. Her palms become sweaty as excitement now takes control of her emotions. She responds, "Ja Charlie, ek sal met jou trou, but ek dink ons moet dit stadig vat, ons altwee het seer gekry, ons moet seker wees." Charlie, taken aback by her response, questions her. "Soe jy willie engage raak met my nie?"

"Charlie moettie silly wiesie of course will ek, ons gaan nie soema trou nie, ons leer ken mekaar eers beter. Sit daai ring op my vinger Charles." Charlie puts the ring on her finger but is also struggling a bit, he never took her actual finger size. He only guessed the size of her finger, as he viewed various rings at the store, this ring caught his eye, even though it was expensive, he is prepared to pay it off over the next 24 months. Sam, amused by the fact that Charlie is struggling to get the ring on her finger, giggles and says, "Charlie my vingers het bietjie duk geraak."

He leaves the ring where it got stuck and replies to Sam, "Moettie worry nie baby, ek kan dit terug neem na die store next week om dit groter te maak." As they continue their journey home, he receives a call from his Aunty Rosie, who is checking up on him only to respond, "Ek is saam met my Fiancé." They smile at each other, as an acknowledgment of their decision. The romantic sounds of Babyface in the car, adding some ambiance to the moment.

A few days later Charlie realizes that, he needs to be a true man and ask Aunty Charlene if he may marry Sam. The mother, being old school and traditional, is a bit disappointed that Charlie had not consulted her first, tells Charlie, "Ek's kwaad vir jou but ek's bly dat jy en Sam saam is. Jy maak haar happy Charlie, julle het my blessing."

The new couple is so excited about the blessing and already talks about the wedding plans and ideas they both have while celebrating with a Bona Vienna & Chips parcel followed by biscuits Sam baked.

Sam informs Charlie that both his daughters must be part of the bridal procession, but he is not very sure about that idea. He wants a small, intermit wedding at Wynberg Court followed by a celebratory lunch at The GrillFather in Woodstock. They still have time to decide and will ponder on the finer details at a later stage.

Charlie never asked Sam about her previous marriage. It never bothered him, but it has been on her mind to tell him what has happened so that there are no secrets between these two lovers. He now needs to know about her past so that he can understand her better. Charlie knows it's the second time around for both of them. As the man, he needs to step up, he wants to give Sam a better life and they need to purchase a house in Grassy Park. A place to call home. Sam is not really about material things, her previous marriage taught her a very valuable lesson. Charlie, on the other hand, feels he wants to give her the best life possible and already thinking of studying to improve his future. He wants to be a better husband to Sam and will do anything in his power to do so.

Sam: "Charlie moettie dinge oordoen nie my skat."
Charlie: "Hoe mean Jy Sam?"

Sam: "Een ding op 'n tyd Charlie, jy hoef my nie meer te impress nie, ek's mos klaar joune Charles." (Loving smile).

It was one morning on their way to work in the taxi when Boeta Iekie asked Charlie, "Hoekom move jy nie in by haar nie?"
Charlie: "Ons is noggie op daai level nie Boeta Iekie."
Boeta Iekie: "Ek en my motjie het eerste in gemove, voor ons getrou het."
Charlie: "But is daai nie tien Boeta Iekie se religion nie?"
Boeta Iekie: "Ja, geen sex voor marriage mos."
Charlie: "Ek sien." He thinks to himself, die bra lieg, hy's baie jas, but that made him think about the idea.
Boeta Iekie: "Is een ding om te spean but 'n ander om te trou."

Sam sitting next to the two, listening to the whole conversation while Boeta Iekie is watching her cleavage and making her feel uncomfortable.

When the taxi stops Sam asks Charlie:
Sam: "Het jy gesien hoe hou Iekie my tette dop, die blerrie ou man."
Charlie can't help to laugh at Sam as she is a bit upset about it.

Like most men, Charlie asks a few of his colleagues at work, what their views are on moving in together before marriage. His one colleague, Aunty Doreen, hears his conversation and wants to share her opinion. She calls him one side and chat with him like a mother would with her son.

Aunty Doreen: "Charlie, jy doen al klaar die stoute deeds," she smiles and continues, "hoekom try jy dit nie net uit nie en maak seker die is wat jy wil hê." Like everyone else, she is also aware of Charlie's previous marriage. He is much happier now that he is with Sam and always up for a challenge.

Charlie's mind is made up, but he also thinks about Sam's words to Him.
Sam: "Ons moet dinge stadig vat." But thinks of the adventures they will have in the bedroom. Deep intimacy, mmmmmmm.

Where Sam, on the other hand, realizes that she is still married and needs to get divorced first if she wants to marry Charlie. This means she will have to face her past one more time. Tony has moved on already but legally they are still married. Sam thinking, hoe maak ek nou, ek gaan nou weer ou koeie uit die sloot grawe. And what if he refuses to give me a divorce?

That afternoon, the two love birds meet, and Sam tells Charlie to rather take the bus.
Sam: "Ons moet praat Charlie."
Sam: "Djy wiet innie taxi luister almal na jou conversation."

They wait for the bus from Mowbray to Wynberg and she opens the conversation.
Sam: "Charlie, ek moet jou iets balangrik sê." Charlie can hear in her tone this sounds serious; he thinks she wants to break up.
Charlie: "Wat pla jou Sam?"
Sam: "Charlie ek is nog nie geskei nie." A sense of shock overcomes Charlie, followed by fear and disappointment. Feels like a whirlwind just took his last breath away. He thinks, what if she never gets a divorce. That means they would never be able to move on.
Charlie: "En nou Samantha, hoe nou?"
Sam: "Ek moet my Ex gaan sien, ek het gedink dus a chapter wat toe is in my lewe?"

Charlie pushes his chest to the front and moves his shoulders up in a stance like that of a bodybuilder, but he looks more like a puffed-up chicken.
Sam: "Ek gaan kontak maak met Tony en hom vra vir 'n divorce."

Charlie, hearing the name "Tony" for the first time, starts wondering about this infamous guy.
Charlie: Wat is sy van?
Sam: "Tony Cupido, Charlie. Tony die vark Cupido," as tears rolls down her cheek.

CHAPTER 7
Cape Point

Charlie and Sam decided it was time to build memories, as the ones they have, is a bit bruised. They decide to spend the day at Cape Point. A place Charlie never knew existed. Sam, on the other hand, use to visit it regularly with her mom and brother when they were younger.

Sunday morning the couple is on their way driving past Simons town. Everything just seems more beautiful when you are happier, the two enjoy the view and stop a few times to appreciate the beauty of nature as they make their way to Cape Point.

They arrived at the gate and enter into the Cape Point Reserve. Sam getting a bit emotional.
Sam: "Charlie die is waar ons as kinders gekom het met my ma."
Charlie: "Dit lyk mooi hier, dus hoekom dit seker so duur is om hier in te kom."
Sam: "Ek het nogals expensive taste Sir Charles," she flirts with him. They turned into Bordjiesdrif and park the car. People are already braaing and swimming.
Charlie takes out the umbrella, blanket and sets it up so he and Sam can sit comfortably.

Charlie wanted to bring his daughters with as Sam suggested, because she wanted to spend time with the two, but Janine don't want them near Sam. The couple speak about the future and how they have to make this work, there are a lot of people that are waiting for their relationship to fail.

Sam: "Charlie moettie worry, oor ander mense nie, as jy gaan lewe vir ander mense se opinions dan gaan ons definitely fail Charlie."

Sam always wanted to be naughty in the bushes and has a surprise for Charlie before they leave the reserve. Charlie getting the braai ready and wanting to make sure he impressed Sam by not over braaing the meat. The two then enjoying the food and Sam gets excited as she eats the wors.

Sam: "Die is daarom duk wors Charlie," as she puts it in her mouth trying to seduce Charlie.

Charlie also getting very excited saying, "Ja dit is Sam." as his heart starts to race with a smile as he looks at her.

Sam: "Ek het niks onder my rok aan nie Charlie, ek sit kaal hier, wat gat jy maak."
Her see-through yellow dress shows the bra and panty she had on this morning was also removed, this happened while Charlie was braaing.

Charlie: "Hiers nog baie mense Sam, ons kan byrrie huis vanaand dit doen, en dit is meer safer."

Sam: "Sê maar nou ons gat dood voor vanaand dan wat Charlie?" He thinks about what Sam is saying and let go of the fear. Sam and he goes for a walk to the side where there is no people, behind a big tree Sam touches his pleasure stick and he gets an instant erection and puts both his hands on Sam's bum cheeks feeling the softness of her peaches. He started to kiss her full lips, it's nice and reminds him of that soft Woolworths sweets. Sam now gets on the ground in the thick grass moving her dress up telling Charlie, "Sit dit in, ek wag Charles, ek wag vir jou." Charlie do as she commands moves his Kappa tracksuite downwards and feeling in charge of this boat ride. She moved the top of the dress to the middle as well so that Charlie can touch her watermelons and enjoy what she has to offer.

As the two reach their destination an aunty walks past with her grandchild and says, "Julle kan die mos byrrie toilets doen, nie in die walkway nie." Charlie and Sam laid as if nothing happened. As the aunty dissapears, the two get dressed and move towards their car, pack up everything and leave the reserve. Sam only starts laughing in the car as Charlie starts to make fun of the situation.
Charlie: "Ek het amper gesê ouma dus Sam wattie wil waggie."
Sam: "At least het jy dit enjoy Charlie, nuwe memories my skat."
Charlie: "Ja, dus blerrie exciting en die wat loer kry niks." The two starts laughing nonstop.

As Charlie drives home, he feels something biting his private parts, he tells Sam. It gets worse as he stops the car and tells Sam, "Dus bal byters wat my byt." Sam is crying as she's laughing at Charlie, she shouts, "Charlie maak hulle dood, wil jy help hê?"

Charlie: "Die goed willie dood nie?" He moves to the side of the car with a bottle of water rinsing his private parts.
Charlie: "At least as os dit weer doen Sam maak seker ons het "a swart sak," and he starts laughing.
Sam: "Is part van die experience Charlie, die memories..."

The couple takes a slow drive home as they witness the beautiful sunset as they drive from Cape Point to Parkwood.

CHAPTER 8
Valentine's Day

Charlie decides to spoil Sam for Valentine's Day.
After all, it is their first Valentine's together and why not make it special, he thinks. He always saw this scene in the movies, where the couple lay in front of the fireplace, on the floor with some scattered rose petals leading to the bathroom, a glass of red wine and music playing in the background. But the reality of the situation is that Sam does not drink and "hulle hettie 'n fire plekkie nie." He also thinks he must make sure that the thorns of the roses are removed, "anderste stiek daai goettes op sy sterre." Sam on the other hand just wants a nice and cozy evening at home.

Sam: "Charlie, Jy kan mos 'n lekker movie vir ons download vir Valentine's Day, 'n romantic eene."
Charlie: "Wil jy nie uit gaan vir 'n drive eerste nie Sam?"
Sam: "Big girls hou mossie eintlik meer Valentine's nie, ons create dit Charles."
Charlie: "Mmm ek likes daai, ek sal likes om 'n memory te create op Signal Hill."

Charlie calls his friend to find out if he can borrow the Golfie for the night, but unfortunately, his friend had other commitments. He wants to take Sam out so desperately that he asks his cousin John aka "Gryssie" as they call him for help. He was the only family member beside Uncle Trevor that still had time for Charlie. Gryssie is that cousin in the family you can depend on any time of the day or night. He's always dodging the law. Gryssie was a real hustler, from smokkeling krief to a blikkie bake beans and most of the time it was stolen goods.

He drove a 1985 Ford Sierra XR6, a maroon one. That car was like a laundry basket, you could find women's underwear anywhere in the car, at any given time. Gryssie always joked, "As die kar kan praat, dan was a paar huwelike al oor." Gryssie lived in Ottery, well known amongst the people because he was known as the, "Vis Man", he was also called, "Jack of all trades but a master at none". Charlie knew he could rely on his cousin and made that call.

Charlie: "Hi Gryssie."

Gryssie had a very deep voice like that bra of Boyz II Men. When he did not recognize the voice or the number calling him, he would answer his cell undercover, "Hello is Danny how can I help you?" Charlie: "Issie die Boerre nie is jou nief Charlie." Recognizing his cousin's voice, Gryssie gets excited!

Gryssie: "Awe Cuz, jy's daarom skaars nou wat jy in love is."
Charlie: "Ja broer jy ken mos, man try maar om 'n goeie mens te wies."
Gryssie: "Is reg Cuzzie, moettie die kak aanvang wat ek aanvang nie," he giggles.
Charlie: "Cuz ek wil vir Tony leen asseblief man, vir Valentine's Day." Tony was the name of Gryssies car, named after the gangster series, 'Tony Soprano'. For some reason, Gryssie thought he was a mafia boss with his imaginary friends.

Gryssie: "Is reg broer, ek gat met 'n ander goose, sy het haar eie kar, 'n Audi broer, Ek speel nourie game," feeling very chuffed with himself.
Charlie: "Ek hoep jy trek 'n jacket (condom) aan, jy het oek elke week 'n ander vrou."
Gryssie: "Broer ek kannie help nie, die vrouens likes my."
Charlie: "Ek is af op Valentine's Day, soe ek kom die kar vroeg haal."
Gryssie: "Ek gat jou wag Cuzzie en kykkie jy moet petrol in gooi, daai kar bly dors."
Charlie: "Ek het geld broer, sal die tank vol maak."

The two said their good-byes but Charlie's mind is working overtime. He's not very sure where he wants to take Sam for Valentine's Day. It has to be a special place.

Everyone goes to fancy clubs in Town, spending a lot of money on drinks they cannot even pronounce, then they still pay it off over 24 months. Charlie took leave for Valentine's Day. He needs to make sure his plans are put into place perfectly. He took a taxi to Ottery from Parkwood to collect the car from Gryssie. Charlie was on "cloud nine" to discover his cousin had taken the car to be washed and the inside was clean.

Gryssie: "Charlie moetie doen wat ekkie sal doennie, but as jy dit moet doen voor in die cubby-hole is protection Cuz."
Charlie: "Thanks Gryssie ek sal dit onthou, sal die kar Sondag bring vir jou."
Gryssie: "Hou die kar ek sal dit kom haal innie week."

Charlie drives away slowly knowing that this could become an expensive experience. He gets an idea, he heard of a club in Mitchells Plain called, Las Vegas Lounge, he always wanted to go there. He heard the vibe was great and maybe afterwards get a bottle of champaigne, take a midnight cruise to Hout Bay and watch the sunrise.

He thinks out loud to himself, "Charlie jy's mos kak romantic bro." He first stops at Civic Barber in Grassy Park to get himself a fader. Let me tell you something if you never had a fader as an uncle on the Cape Flats, you have never really experienced the art of a true creative hair artist.

After the barber, he went home to Sam. He drives through Blackbird Avenue to get to the court and revs the car so that Sam must hear he is outside. Instead, the Aunty in Edna Court shouts, "Pop it, Charlie! Pop it!" He is tempted but he knows it is not his car and rather switches off the ignition. As Charlie enters the doorway, Sam asks him, "En nou Charlie, jy's weer lekker rodomontade nuh?" using a big word which confuses Charlie.

Charlie: "Rommel watte Sam?"
Sam: "Rodomontade Charles, dus maar net 'n synonym vir brekgat," she giggles.
Charlie: "Ek gaan oek maar beginte lees saam met jou, jy ken oek baie woorde Miss Clever."

Finally, it is that time to get the Valentine's groove on. The two are dressed, complimenting each other. Sam wearing a white summer dress and Charlie has on a Cuban style shirt and Cuban style pants with a pair of biscuit Grassies.

Charlie: "Jy lyk stunning Sam."
Sam: "Dankie Charles, jy lyk self nie bad nie, but dink jy nie is te laat vir 'n paar Ray-Bans nie? Ek mean manet, 'n Ford Sierra XR6 met Ray-Bans en 'n paar Grassies. Hulle dink netma jy's 'n merchant wat escape het vannie 1980s." Sam laughs as she knows Charlie still loves to wear clothing brands from the '80s and '90s.

Charlie: "Jy kan maar nou ophou Sam", as he sings the song, "Bringing sexy back".

The two leave the Parkwood area and head for Las Vegas Lounge in Mitchells Plain. The car just cruising down Old Strandfontein Road into Spine road. Gryssie forgot his CD in the CD player. "At least it is not a panty," Charlie jokes. He presses the play button, the sounds of "Cherish" by Kool & the Gang fills the air.

Sam: "Die is een van my favourite numbertjies Charlie."
Charlie: "Myne oek, nou is dit ons sinne."

Tony, the car, pulls up in the parking lot of Las Vegas Lounge and the couple exit the car, while the bouncers watch them. The place is packed but the couple is there to enjoy themselves. Charlie sees a few familiar faces at the bar and greets them. The DJ is getting the crowd all hyped up as he spins the decks. Charlie, feeling the music and the party vibe, starts dancing as a familiar song plays, "Trust and believe" by Keyshia Cole. Sam is on the dance floor with Charlie. All eyes are on them, as you can immediately sense they have not been in a club for a long time. But they are entertaining the crowd and eventually everyone is on the dance floor. One of the owners decides to give the couple a bottle of Johny Black as an incentive for getting the crowd on the floor.

Sam: "Charlie ons drink die vanaand byrrie huis."
Charlie: "Hoekom nie nou nie Sam?"

Sam: "Ons is mos responsible Charlie."
Charlie: "But Johny Black maak jou mossie dronk nie."
Sam: "Charlie ons kan drink but kom ons doen dit byrrie huis, asseblief skat," in her flirtatious voice.
Charlie: "Ok Samantha."

The evening was great, and the atmosphere was awesome in the club, a perfect "let your hair down" evening. It is 1am and the couple need to get ready to go home. Charlie decides he is going to do what his cousin Gryssie does, park somewhere and get a bit "ouderwets" He decides to park on Boyes Drive where the Shark Watchers normally stand. A few other cars are also parked a few meters away from them with steamed windows.

Sam: "Ek wonne hoekom is die mense se karre so op ge-steam."
Charlie: "Miskien grill hulle mekaar innie kar," laughing out loud.
Sam: "Hahahaha Charlie, jy kan daarom baie vespot wies as jy tyd het, but wanne grill jy vir my Charlie?" And she lifts her dress and put his hand on her right thigh, his favorite spot.
Charlie: "Jassis Sam, jy't daarom 'n lekker paar boure," and he touches it and feels her soft smooth skin.

The two starts kissing each other. Sam's full lips are in full control of Charlie's lips. They feel the passion, inhaling and exhaling deep breaths of lust as the car's windows start to fog up, just like the other cars around them. Sam lower the seat so that she could lay down while Charlie gets on top of her. Remembering Gryssie's words, "My broer daar is protection innie cubby-hole" but he is already in Sam's mall. Doing his shopping, starting to run down the aisle as his heart is now at maximum rate.

Sam starts to moan and calls his name softly, "Charlie." This turns him on, but he can no longer control himself. He tells Sam to just relax, he needs to put on a life jacket. Sam allows Charlie to do his thing. They need to be safe and protected even if she did not want him to remove his trolley. It was a mutual decision, to be a responsible couple. Charlie gets ready to continue, he gets into shopping mode in Sam's mall. He loads his trolley and as he gets ready to pay his load, he hears a knock on the car's window. The black tinted windows did not allow anyone to see into the car.

Charlie jumps back into the driver's seat and pulls up his pants while Sam moves the seat up. The two wait a few minutes, while Charlie switches the cars ignition on,
just in case he needs to get away in a hurry. The person knocks again, and Charlie rolls down the window slightly. He looks into the face of a white man surrounded by a few ladies. The man introduces himself. "Hi, I am Bryan, we are from the Neighbourhood Watch and just wanted to let you guys know it's a bit dangerous here this time of the night."

Charlie: "Hi Bryan thanks for the warning, this is my girlfriend Samantha and my name is Charlie."
Bryan: "Not a problem Sir, take care now. Everyone else greets the couple and move along to the next car.
Sam: "Die mense is nogals nice en decent Charlie."
Charlie: "Ja hulle is nice but hy kan mos net 'n bietjie gewag het voor hy geklop het, ek het amper 'n deposit gemaak," he giggles.

They decide to go home and rather continue the shopping adventure in the privacy of their bedroom. The maroon Ford Sierra drives home playing some George Benson as you hear the sound of v6 power taking them home. Sam thanks Charlie for a lovely evening, it was something to treasure. "Charlie jy was oulik vanaand baie dankie jy laat my baie special voel."

Charlie: "Jy maak my happy Samantha, ek's lief vir jou.

CHAPTER 9
Tony Cupido

Tony, a financial advisor and like Aunty Charlene would say, "Glat mettie bek," was Sam's high school sweetheart. The two met when they were in Standard 8 at Steenberg High School. Tony had his Western Province colors and could run like the wind. In fact, their meeting was accidental. A boy stole Sam's calculator and she went to report it at the office. Tony was sitting there waiting to see the principle who wanted to speak to him about his low grades.

It was love at first sight, Sam had a very long ponytail back then and Tony made his move. After a few intervals she was all his. Aunty Charlene was not very happy that Sam now had a boyfriend, she struggled to raise Sam and her brothers as a single parent. Sam's dad was a part-time musician and one night did not come home after a gig, he went to go play on another lady's strings and later married her. Tony always wanted to impress Sam.

Tony: "Ek gat die vinnigste colored man innie Kaap wies."
Sam: "Lekker Tony." It's here where she developed the habit of giggling if something was funny or if she did not know how to reply.

Both Sam and Tony finished school. Sam did a two-year Travel and Tourism course and wanted to explore her country, but this never happened. She could not find employment and rather started working in a call centre.

Tony on the other hand never became a runner because after school he did not continue in athletics and picked up weight. "Kan mossie soos 'n Oros mannetjie lyk en die vinnigste man innie Kaap wil wiesie." He had to settle for a job in the financial industry, selling policies and because of his smooth mouth, he did really well.

After two years of selling policies, just on the commission he made, he had a deposit for a house. This now means he wanted to get married and start a family. One night after watching a movie with Sam, he took out a ring, went on his knees and said, "Samantha sal jy met my trou?" Sam never expected this but could not say no either. The two had been together for a while and he was her first boyfriend.

Sam: "Sjoe Tony jy speel oekkie, but ja ek sal met jou trou."

Aunty Charlene was angry because Tony never asked her if he could propose, sy was old school en respek was important. Charlene could see her Sam was happy and that is all that mattered to her, the happiness of her children.

This was going to be the wedding of the century! Tony was baie bragerig and always wanted to impress people. He took out a loan for the wedding and purchased a flat in Kuilsriver for them. Tony's mantra was "If you can dream it you must achieve it."

The wedding had all the bells and whistles, a live band, a Rolls Royce was hired, the honeymoon was in Sun City, Johannesburg, and the tickets were booked by SAA.

Two years after the wedding, things changed, Tony developed a gambling problem and owed the Sherrif money. Sam could not have children according to him and he started beating her. Some days Sam had to stay home because she had a blue eye. The Tony she met was no longer. Some evenings dodgy people will come to the flat and give Tony bags full of money to invest.

The fairy tale turned into a horror movie. Aunty Charlene picked up on what was happening and already saw the bruises on her daughter's arms. She had to step in otherwise, Sam will not get out alive. Tony was also sleeping around. He became very dark inside.

The Tony Sam knew was gone. One day, Aunty Charlene came to fetch her daughter and it was a fight, she was not leaving Sam behind. The neighbours called the cops and within five minutes they were there. Sam all bruised and wearing a T-shirt was taken to the police station for a statement. Tony was locked up that day, but his connection made the docket disappear.

Sam resigned from her job and she and her mother bought a flat in Parkwood. Sam had to disappear, who knows what Tony would to do her. She had to go for counselling, she was a nervous wreck no more smiles, low self-esteem and she even wrote a suicide note. Aunty Charlene a retired nurse looked after her daughter, and after a year you could see the old Sam was returning.

Aunty Charlene made sure her daughter knew that she was there for her. Sam developed a low self-esteem because of her experience and did not trust men because of Tony's abuse. She started blaming herself more often, maybe if she were a better wife and made herself prettier this would never had happened. Many nights she could not sleep and wanted to go back to Tony and apologise to him for being a bad wife, but Aunty Charlene made sure that Sam knew it was not her fault and that she should not feel guilty about anything.

CHAPTER 10

The Aftermath

Sam was alone at home taking a bath while Charlie took Chester for a walk. The face cloth was over her head and she was relaxing in the bath. It was load shedding as per normal, Sam's phone was playing some music and she was enjoying the moment, with some red wine Charlie brought home from work.

In her mind she was thinking how blessed she is and how her life use to be, appreciating Charlie and the way he loved her. She heard the front door opening and ask, "Charlie is dit djy?" No answer, maybe she is imagining herself. She thinks to herself, wie sal dan nou inbriek by die council huisie, is mossie soes innie movies nie. She starts laughing.

She continues to lay in the bath with no bathroom door, Charlie was supposed to get one of the carpenter uncles to fix the door. The music continued to play, and she relaxed again. Suddenly she felt two hands on her neck, choking her, trying to drown her. Anxiety kicks in and Sam is fighting for her life, she can't see who the person is that is trying to kill her.

She managed to get him off, gets up but she slips again in the bath, this time laying with her head down.
The person keeps her under water. She starts losing consciousness and prays that Charlie and Chester retruns home soon. Waar is Charlie, Here laat hy my net kom save asseblief!

She hears Charlies voice as he is telling her, "Is ok Sam, dit was net 'n droem." It felt so real, just like the other dreams she had expierenced the last few months.
Charlie ask Sam to go see a professional, but she do not see the need.

Sam: "Ons coloreds worry mossie om shrinks te sien nie Charlie, ons sort mos alles uit onse self."
Charlie: "Daai issie problem baby, daai is hoekom baie mense nooit healing kry nie. Dit het vir my gewerk en ek het tools geleer om my issues te manage."
Sam: "Het jy 'n shrink gesien Charlie?"
Charlie: "Ja ek het. Die ding met Anton het my lewe begin oorvat, toe het ek iemand gesien en dit het my baie gehelp, ek sal even saam met jou gaan Sam."
Sam: "Maybe moet ek dit net try."
Charlie: "Jy't niks om te verloor nie. My verlede het my amper opgevriet en rejection het gemaak dat ek suicide wou commit."
Sam: "Ek wil hê jy moet saam met my gaan, nuh Charlie?" Charlie: "Of course sal ek met jou gaan."

The counselling helped Sam a lot and the dreams were becoming less frequent as she made progress. She realised your body does not only need healing outside, but it is important that you heal inside as well.

CHAPTER 11
Moving In

Arriving from Goudini Spa the two decide to move in together, see how things work out before they really commit. Aunty Charlene decided to move to her son in Elsies River and let Sam and Charlie live in the flat and see if the two are ready to move on with their lives.

While sitting in the dining room after lunch, Charlie duk geeët van Sam se hoender, geel rys en aartapels.
 Sam: "Charlie trou issie perde koep nie, ons altwee was al klaar daar."

Charlie, while drinking his bieka of coffee, "Is waar Sam, ons enjoy lieweste elke dag en leer ken mekaar eerste."

In a very relaxing afternoon mode while the radio is playing jazz the two speak about this and that. Charlie tells Sam he has a deposit for a car and that they should buy one especially when she works late shifts, as he can not always borrow his friends' cars. They both agreed.

Sam: "Ja dan kan ons lekker uit gaan weekends."
Charlie: "Ja, en die kar inseën." The two get erotic ideas as they think about it.

They hit the road month end in a taxi to go look for a car.
Sam: "Gat jy 'n Golfie koep Charlie?"
Charlie: "Die seats issie soe comfortable nie, vir wat ons in mind het nie." He looks in her eyes and realise what a gem she is. She does everything with him, as he compares her to Janine.

Sam: "Moet nie ons compare nie, sy is nog die ma van jou kinders Charles."

They continue searching for a car but find nothing. Not in a hurry as well, they leave the search for another day. While living together the two realise that although they are deeply inlove with each other they work on each other's nerves from time to time. Sam is very neat, and Charlie is totally the opposite.

Sam: "Ek kan mossie altyd wil optel agter jou nie."
Charlie: "Hoekom draai jy altyd so, ek moet altyd vir jou wag."

They cannot afford to live like this and need to get help. They decide to go for counselling, it will help them to understand each other and learn new tools. After a few sessions at one of the local churches, things already start looking better. The insecurities from the previous relationships had carried over and the emotional scars are still very real.

With the counseling things are going better. The two now learn how to compliment each other. It is still very new to them but a challenge they are willing to accept, as the Pastor and his wife told them during counselling.

"As Charlie poep en jy hou nie van dit nie, moet jy hom sê Sam, en wanneer Sam se kos miskien te veel sout in het moet jy haar sê Charlie." A relationship is special, and communication is key. The pastor couple has been married for more than forty- five years and the wisdom shows in their conversations and grey hair. The years has changed the two's appearance, but the spark is definitely still there. Pastor Michael still opens the car door for his wife, Cecilia.

One Saturday afternoon after counselling Charlie saw Pastor helping his wife putting on her coat that was so beautiful. He and Janine never did it. Sam gets a flashback of her ex-husband Tony, he used to do that to her, but it stopped when he started beating her. Charlie takes her hand and tells her, "Daai gaan ons twee wees eendag Sam."
Sam: "Ja Charlie, ons twee moet saam oud word," reminiscing of the pain of a previous marriage, she kisses him on his cheek. The car is not a necessity now, they will rather wait for the right moment to buy a car.

Sam: "Charlie ek het eendag gehoor, iemand praat oor Needs and Wants, en dit was nogals interesting."
Charlie: "Nou maak vir my oek slim Samantha?"

Sam: "Is simple Charlie, jy koep wat jy nodig het, nie wat jy wil hê nie. Byvoorbeeld, wat is meer belangrik skoene of 'n kar? As jy nie skoene het nie?"
Charlie: "Obviously 'n kar om die skoene te gaan koep."
Sam: "Nee Charlie, jy's verkeerd," as she wants to burst out from laughter.
Sam: "Charlie sekere goed in onse lewe is net luxury, ons is so gespoil dat ons wil net die beste van alles hê en vergeet wat het ons regtig nodig in die lewe."
Charlie: "Ek speel net Sam, but jy is reg. Ons moet spaar saam lewe ek wil jou eendag oppie MSC boat vat virre cruise nog."
Sam: "Daai sal lekker wies Charlie, kom ons maak dit happen."
Charlie: "Ons kan elke maand spaar, minder take ways koop einde van die maand en miskien kan ons die geld gebruik vir 'n deposit."
Sam: "Daar is jy alweer verkeerd Charlie, ons moet spaar."
Charlie: "Ja, ja, ja Sam, ons spaar."

CHAPTER 12
The Divorce

Sam tracked Tony and had to see him in order to ask him to sign the divorce papers. She wanted to meet Tony on her own, but Charlie insisted he wants to go along even if he had to sit and wait outside. Charlie had other plans, he wanted to teach this Tony guy a lesson and already arranged with his old buddy David to go with, just in case he needs backup or help.
Sam: "Charlie hoeko vat jy ander mense saam om my battle te baklei?"
Charlie: "Just in case daai Tony se brasse is oek daar."
Chester his dog was also in the car.

Charlie managed to borrow his friend's car, a white Honda Vtec. "Tony moet sien ons het oek," he tells himself.

Tony now living in Walmer Road, Woodstock did not expect what was about to happen. On their way to Woodstock, Charlie starts playing Tupac's music to get him in a mood for this Tony 'bra'. As they drive towards Woodstock everyone is quiet, and you can sense everyone has something on their minds.

Sam: (deep in thought) "Ek wil mossie vandag die jong sien nie, sê ma nou hy willie skei nie, dan wat?"
Charlie: (thinks deeply) "Vandag moer ek 'n bra, hy slat mos vroumense. Los hom, hy't my noggie in action gesien nie, plus ek en David het al baie manne saam pak gegee al."
David: (thinks deeply) "Wat maak ek hier, die issie eers my battle nie, plus ek is self innie kak. Jessica is pregnant en my motjie gat uitvind binnekort, after all, hulle is niggies." Dit lyk asof die hond Chester oek diep in gedagte is. Miskien mis hy Charlie se twee dogters, hulle het elke oggend vir hom 'n soentjie gegee.

They arrive in Walmer Road and Sam ask Charlie to behave and wait in the car. She goes to the white door and knocks. She waits a few minutes and a lady opens the door. Sam greets and says, "Ek soek vir Tony."

The lady asks for her name and Sam replied, "My naam is Samantha Cupido." The lady asked, "Is jy Tony se suster of niggie, jy lyk nogals soes hy?" Sam replied, "Ek is sy vrou en ek wil 'n divorce hê, kan jy hom roep asseblief!"

The lady was quiet, shocked, and disappointed, Tony was living with her for almost two years now and never told her that he was still married. She shouts, "Tony jou vrou is hier!"

Tony makes his way from the room and sees Sam standing at the front door, not knowing what to say. He asks her, "Wat wil jy hê?"

Sam: "Ek wil 'n divorce hê, jy moet die papiere sign, dan is ons klaar met mekaar."

Tony: "Jy kom hier om my die kak te vra," trying to embarrass her one more time.
Sam: "Ek willie nog stry nie, sign net die papiere asseblief en jy sal my nooit weer sien nie."

He tells Sam that she has to pay him for his signature.
Sam: "Jou vark na alles wat jy aan my gedoen het wil jy my nog threaten?"

The lady standing next to Tony starts wondering about this guy she allowed into her home. He seemed like a sweet guy but the way he is speaking to Sam now makes her wonder if this is really what she wants.
Sam not going to allow Tony to intimidate her, tells Tony, "As jy nie die papiere nou sign nie, laat ek daai twee gangsters wat innie kar sit jou bene briek," pointing in the direction of the white Honda Vtec that is now playing loud Tupac numbertjies. Tony looks out and catches the grim on Charlie's face.

Tony: "Wat bring jy gangsters na my huistoe?"
She reminds him of how he brought gangsters and prostitutes into their home, how he used to beat her and lock her up. The other lady's mind is made up after

she hears what Sam says and will be kicking Tony out after Sam leaves. Tony grabs the paper, "Waar sign ek?" Sam: "Daar waar die kruisie is, en initial elke page." Tony takes the papers inside and comes back five minutes later with signed papers.

Sam: "Dankie Tony en enjoy die res van jou miserable lewe," as she walks towards her new future waiting in the white Vtec.

She gets in the car and tells Charlie, "Die papiere is gesign, kom ons gaan McDonald's toe om the celebrate. Ek is single nou Charles," causing everyone in the car to laugh.

Tony had to move out, the lady got an interdict against him as well, after hearing Sam's story she decided Tony is no longer welcome to live with her any longer.

CHAPTER 13

The Wedding

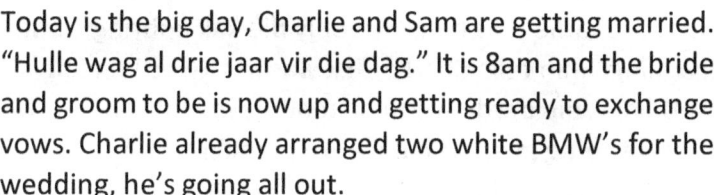

Today is the big day, Charlie and Sam are getting married. "Hulle wag al drie jaar vir die dag." It is 8am and the bride and groom to be is now up and getting ready to exchange vows. Charlie already arranged two white BMW's for the wedding, he's going all out.
His friend Jason will DJ and it is important that Kenny G's song, "Forever" is playing when they walk in.

The drivers were told, "Julle moet ons Claremont Gardens toe vat virrie photos." The court wedding became a Cape Flats wedding. Charlie invited his estranged brother and father, not sure, if they will be there, but it was Sam's idea. She told him, "Charlie invite jou pa en jou broer." Charlie was not very happy about this idea, as he had to live with his uncle Trevor when his mother died, his father, Anton, did not want anything to do with him.

Charlies grey suite was bought at Markhams, his black Crockett & Jones at Harringtons and the shirt and tie was on a special at Edgars. Excited and happy to start a new chapter in his life. It's 12pm and the car came to fetch him and his best man, Stan. They were school friends and Stan was a fisherman always at sea.

The white BMW with the pink ribbon takes Charlie and Stan to the church in 3rd Avenue. Charlie reckons to Stan "My broe ek's mos kak nervous," with a frown on his face. Stan, the funny guy comforts Charlie, "My broer jy's 'n expert in die," and they all laugh at his best buddy. Charlie tells him, "Moet jy die kak opbring," both laughing. Stan tells Charlie, "Ek was in altwee van jou weddings, die derde wedding moet jy my fokken present terug gee." The guys are breaking themselves with laughter and enjoying their silly talk.

Stan: "Charlie my broer, ons moet in gaan, but ek wil jou net happiness wens ou bra, jy verdien baie geluk."
Charlie: "Dankie my broer, ek waardeer dit."

As the two friends, enter the church, the DJ start playing the wrong song. Charlie upset, showing the DJ with his finger to play number five. The guests stand up and welcomes the groom-to-be. The two guys are seated in the front now, waiting for Sam and her girls. The DJ is playing some Kenny Latimore music while they are waiting.

Sam getting dressed and asking her two bridesmaids to help her with her dress. Valerie an old school friend and Carmen, her cousin, are with her. Sam worrying about Charlie if he managed to sort out everything. Carmen assures her that Charlie has everything under control.

Carmen: "Moettie stress nie Cuz, jou man het alles organise."
Valerie: "Ja hoeko stress jy, vanaand gat jy en Charlie mos lekker Kilimanjaro klim," all three ladies laughing.

Valerie: "Ek wiettie wanne laas ek berg geklim het nie, ek bly by die blerrie cable car." They laughed so happily that Carmen accidentally farted.

The white BMW is waiting, and the three ladies get into the car and are finally on their way to the church. They arrive at the church and the music starts playing. The DJ has the song wrong again, Charlie agitated tells Stan, "Die bra is fokken onooslik!" Stan smiles and say, "Daai gebeur mos as jy cheap wil wies." Eventually he gets the song right, and beautiful Sam, escorted by her brother Theo, walks into the church. Charlie collects his bride and smiles proudly at Sam.

Charlie: "Jy lyk mooi Samantha..."
Sam: "Dankie Charles, jy lyk handsome in jou suit, my man."

Standing in front of the Church, Pastor Booysen officiates the wedding. He is a very strict pastor and first ask them, "Is julle sieka julle wil die doen?"

The couple looks at each other and both respond, "Ja Pastor."

Pastor Booysen: "Alright laat ons begin." He titles his sermon, "In sickness and in health." Talking about how easily couples give up and that whenever they have a problem not to go sleep and leave it but always try and resolve their issues.

Before he let the two exchange vows, he reads a scripture:

1 Corinthians 13:1 Love is patient, love is kind. It does not envy, it does not boast, it is not proud. It is not rude, it is not self-seeking, it is not easily angered, it keeps no record of wrongs. Love does not delight in evil but rejoices with the truth.

He ends his sermon with, "Julle twee moet mekaar verdra op die pad." He can see Charlie's mind is at the honeymoon stages already.
Pastor Booysen: "Mnr & Mev Daniels, julle is nou wetlik getroud, jy mag jou vrou soen Charles."

Charlie kisses his Sam and tells her, "Djy is my alles."
The register is now being signed and it's finally official. A taxi incident led to a love affair and then to a beautiful marriage.

The cars are on their way to Claremont and the driver is softly playing some Eric Clapton music in the car. Charlie wanted his two daughters to attend his big day, but Janine did not want the kids to attend. He has not seen them for three months and is seeing a lawyer.

He has also been receiving strange calls. Someone calls and breathe loud into the phone and puts down after two minutes. He called the number several times already and says the number does not exist.

He confronted Janine and she denied it, with her eliminated, he wonders who else could it be. They arrive at Claremont Gardens and Sam tells Charlie, "Ons moet 'n photo vat voor die groot boom vir onse voorkamer," both laughing because most Cape Flats couples has a photo of that tree in their homes. It is as if Harry the Strandloper planted that tree there.

Charlie sees an unfamiliar male starring at them the whole time while taking photos.

CHAPTER 14

Wedding Reception

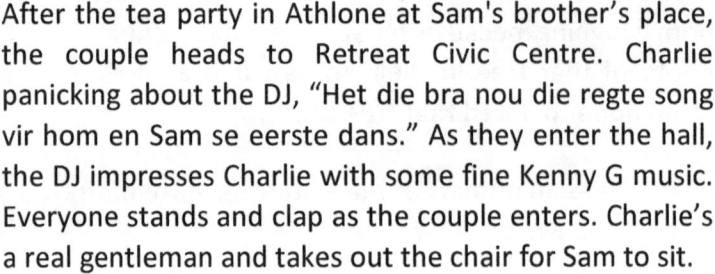

After the tea party in Athlone at Sam's brother's place, the couple heads to Retreat Civic Centre. Charlie panicking about the DJ, "Het die bra nou die regte song vir hom en Sam se eerste dans." As they enter the hall, the DJ impresses Charlie with some fine Kenny G music. Everyone stands and clap as the couple enters. Charlie's a real gentleman and takes out the chair for Sam to sit.

The MC takes the microphone, it is no other than Ballie, Charlie's connection for everything. He cracks a few colored jokes, which is always a winner at colored parties. Aunty Charlene looks very happy and sits next to Sam with her big hat, after all, she is the bride's mother and she has to look the part. Charlie sitting there, neither his brother, father nor children came. He does not want to show it, but he feels hurt and very disappointed. Before he stands up to do his speech, he notices the same person he saw at Claremont Gardens coming straight to him. The person shakes his hand and congratulate him on his big day.

Charlie: "Hello Uncle, van waar is Uncle?" He replies, "Ek's 'n ou vriend van jou ma Mandy."

Sam watching the scenario and notices a resemblance in the two. Charlie did not invite this man and had only paid for the people that is there. Thinking in his mind, die bra bieta line, ek hettie nog 'n kop se geld nie. The man introduces himself as Deon, he remembers his mom and Anton always use to fight about a Deon. "Charlie ek's jou regte pa." Sam overhear those words. She stands next to her man, her new husband.

Charlie looks at this guy and asks him, "Waar was jy al die tyd, my ma en ek was elke dag abused en djy was missing." The civic is quiet as the DJ stoped the music. Charlie: "Dankie dat jy my gewish het but ek mekeer jou definitely nie in my lewe nie."

Ballie walks over to the DJ.
Ballie: "Word jy betaal om net daar te staan? Speel 'n number man."
DJ: "Julle het my nie eers betaal nie," he mumbles but plays "Autumn Leaves". The aunties start to dance on the song and forgot about what just happened.

Sam ask him, "Charles is jy ok?"
Charlie: "Kan jy dit glo, daai bra kom na al die jare en vir my nou daai kak vertel dat hy is my pa."
Sam: "Charlie is ok as jy wil huil, ek is hier vir jou."

The mood has now changed, and they go straight to eating and forget about the rest of the program.

The civic is only booked till 10pm and the caretaker is already busy packing up the chairs. All that matters today is that he married Sam and he is starting over. Charlie wanted to make sure he gives Sam a honeymoon she will never forget. He has saved up a few rands and his bra Ballie who works at the navy, assisted. Ballie was one of those people who had connections everywhere. Ballie got him a few days in Langebaan at Club Mykonos at a cheap rate, in return Charlie had to buy him a bottle Johny Black Label.

After the reception, the couple got a lift with their friend with the Mk1 Golfie, where Charlie had his first taste of honeymoon with Sam. Unfortunately, his friend needs the car for work and was not able to borrow it to them. The couple was now dropped and ready for action. Charlie did not want to disappoint and bought some tablets at the Chinese shop in Ottery.

Vanaand gat hy Sam heel aand slat met sy pleasure stick dink hy. Sam on the other hand was tired, and grateful that she is now finally Mrs Daniels and that the wedding ceremony is over. Charlie remembers the instructions from the guy at the shop where he bought the tablets: "Yu drink the tablet 30 minutes befur yu dho da thang." Charlie dink hy is Danielson in "Karate Kid".

It's almost 12pm, and the two are watching some TV while laying in each others' arms. Charlie goes to the open plan kitchen and get some water from the tap.

Drinking his tablet called the Silver Bullet, he goes back to sit next to Sam. Almost 35 minutes had passed and nothing has happened yet.

Sam: "Charlie kom ons gat slaap is al laat skat."
A worried Charlie not feeling any movement in his pleasure stick is a bit worried, he paid R40 a tablet.

Charlie: "Ek gat gou shower," trying to buy some time. He gets into the shower and a few minutes later, something is happening to him. His stomach starts making funny sounds and he assures himself it is the tablet working. However, he needs to sit on the toilet pot. He gets out of the shower and makes himself comfortable. He releases a gas bomb followed by a few masala missiles.

The strong masala chicken his Aunty Rosie made for the reception got his ass burning and thinks for himself, "Is mos van uitgevriet wil wies."

Worried, Sam asking him, "Charlie is jy ok?"
He mumbles back, "Ja Sammy." His stomach running and disappointed in himself, he stays in the toilet.

Sam laying in the bedroom, dressed in her pink lingerie with a matching pink slipper with fur on, smelling like Coco Chanel, which Charlie bought her. A bit worried she goes to the bathroom and softly asks him, "Wat makeer Charlie?" He tells her, "My mag werk."

She could not help to laugh, "Van wat Charlie?" "Aunty Rosie se hoender", sê Charlie.

Sam makes some strong black coffee while her man is fighting a war of his own. Eventually the war subsides, and Charlie manages to freshen up and rejoin Sam in the dining room and tells her what really happened. Sam was impressed and amused by his attempt to keep the pleasure stick going all night.

Sam: "Charlie jy't my nog nooit disappoint nie, gooi daai pille weg, ons sal more die regte Silver Bullet try." The lesson Charlie learnt was never try to impress anyone and not to purchase tablets from Chinese Shops.

The two go to bed falling asleep. 5am the morning Sam feels Charlie's hand moving up her thighs removing her thong, he gently rubs her genie lamp, and this granting him three wishes. He removes his Bad Boy trunky he bought from Edgars for the honeymoon.

He puts his right hand on her left breast and starts playing with it. Sam now enjoying it and slowly waking up from a deep sleep. She takes off her lingerie, turns around, and tells Charlie, "Kom Chester, ek mean Charlie." He appreciates the view from behind and gives her what she asked for. As he reaches Kilimanjaro, which Sam already did, he tells Sam, "Ek is lief vir jou."

CHAPTER 15

Deon Abrahams

When Mandy, Charlie's mom saw Deon for the first time, it was over. She was in love with him. Deon was good at drawing and was aspiring to be an architect and that is exactly where he ended up, making good money.

Deon loved Mandy but was never ready to commit. His father wanted him to marry Natasha, which he did but after ten years of marriage he divorced her, the two had no children and that was the problem, Deon always wanted kids.

Mandy married Anton and he knew about the history between Deon and Mandy. Deon never forgot about Mandy, she was his first love but because of his father's request, he was forbidden to see Mandy. The two were very close at school, they used to "vry" everytime they saw each other. Every afternoon Deon would carry Mandy's backpack. They lived fifteen mintues away from the school, but the walk was a one hour walk back home. Mandy always had a special place in her heart for Deon. On weekends, the couple would meet skelmpies at Muizenberg Beach just to see each other and spend the day together. They had a very special bond and were soulmates. Their relationship was supposed to last forever and a day. It was in matric when Deon's father chased Mandy away from their home. She was never supposed to visit him or see him. Deon's father was very much about material things and because Mandy came from a poor family and her father was an alcoholic, she was not good enough to uphold the Abraham's family image.

Deon still very young at the time, had no choice but to obey his father and ended the relationship with Mandy. This is where Anton came in and comforted Mandy and promised her he would look after her.

Deon went to UWC finished his degree and worked for a company in Cape Town. He totally forgot about Mandy and moved on with his life. She never forgot about him and sometimes would call him just to hear his voice and put the phone down. Deon had long black hair, always wore a blazer to school and looked like a coloured Greek god from the Cape Flats, according to Mandy.

His lips were soft and the scent he used smelled like he just stepped out of a bath. Mandy always wanted to marry Deon and wanted his children. Little Greek gods from the Cape Flats. The two would participate at school events especially when they could do a duet and look into each other's eyes. And boy could they sing, they had angelic voices and were asked especially on Valentine's Days to perform at school.

The thing that really broke Mandy's heart was that something so beautiful to her was stopped and that Deon's family never approved of it. He moved on within weeks and forgot about Mandy and what they had once shared.

After many years they met at the school reunion and a night of passion turned into a life of abuse for Mandy. Deon knew he was Charlie's father but Mandy didn't want him near Charlie. He had already broken her heart and she only wanted to protect Charlie from getting hurt. Charlie looked and walked just like Deon, there was no doubt that he was Charlie's Father. Anton hated Mandy for doing this to him and every single time he saw Charlie, it reminded him of Deon and Mandy's fling.

Charlie was always excluded from family parties; he never went with to family gatherings. Everyone else also knew about the night at Princess Vlei and that Charlie was not Anton's son. Through all this Mandy taught the boy to always greet Anton and be polite towards Anton. Charlie and his mom shared a room and was not allowed to go into Anton's room. It was one night when Anton was drunk, he forced Mandy to sleep with him. He ripped her clothes off, pushed Charlie against the cupboard in the kitchen as he tried to assist his mom. Charlie was locked up in the toilet while Anton raped her repeatedly saying, "Djy is mos sleg, ek sal jou wys wat ek saam met jou doen jou gintoe." Mandy crying and shouting, "Asseblief Anton hou op?"

He did not stop, nor did he care about the pain she was experiencing, it was revenge for Deon.

A few months later she found out she was pregnant, and this was unexpected. She gave birth to a son and Anton named him Reginald. He was treated differently to Charlie. Anton would spend time with him and buy him gifts while Charlie was ignored and treated like someone with a disease.

What hurt Charlie the most was he never got any gifts on birthdays or Christmas. He was also not allowed to play with Reginald's toys or in his room. Charlie's Uncle Trevor, Mandy's younger brother, knew exactly what was happening and would allow the boy to sleep over and would try and be the father figure in his life. It's here where he met Janine at Uncle Trevor's house. Trevor would fetch the boy every second week if he was not working. This was something Charlie needed and would take him out of the negative environment. Anton would wait for Charlie to arrive home and tell him what an awesome weekend he and Reginald had, and they would do it again if Charlie was not home. How could a grown up do this to a child? Through all this, Charlie did what his mother said, he should be nice to his brother Reggie and respect Anton. Charlie figured out who his father was because his Uncle Trevor told him the story.

CHAPTER 16
Charlie's Daughters

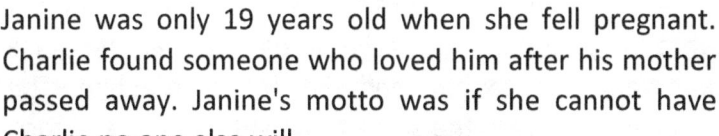

Janine was only 19 years old when she fell pregnant. Charlie found someone who loved him after his mother passed away. Janine's motto was if she cannot have Charlie no one else will.

Charlie's first-born daughter's name is Melony. She was the apple of his eye. Everyone knew Charlie was a good father and spent a lot of time with his daughters. One day, Melony was with her daycare mom. Melony being an innocent, inquisitive, and busy girl, was always mischevious. The daycare mom was very irresponsible and boiled water in the kettle. Melony at the time wandering around in the house went into the kitchen while the daycare mom was in the dining room watching "Days of Our Lives". Melony entered the kitchen and reaching for her bottle, which is normally on the deep freezer, pulls the kettle and spilled the boiling water over her. Her skin started to peel off instantly. The daycare mom panicked and called Charlie's work, explained to him what had happened,
and he should rush home.

No car available for the emergency, he told his manger he needs to get home and described what happened. The manager told him he can not leave and needs to finish his work. He realized they thought nothing of him at work and he took his bag and told the manager to shove her job where the sun does not shine.

He left and rushed home and managed to call an ambulance. He told one of the taxi owners in Wynberg what happened and got a lift straight home. The uncle was very kind to him and did not charge him. The ambulance arrived the same time with Charlie and took the father and daughter to Victoria Hospital.

He stayed with his daughter the whole week while she was in hospital. Janine would just drop fresh clothes at the hospital and could not stay because she worked in the evening and slept during the day. Unemployed Charlie did not worry about a job as he made a promise to God that he will raise his kids with all his love unlike his father Anton.

When Melony turned three years old, another girl was born, and they named her Natalie. She was very shy and had autism. Charlie loved his daughter despite of what people thought. Charlie heard one day from a family friend that his father Anton said the reason his daughter had autism was because of his mother's affair. It was a curse that God punished Charlie with.

Charlie was not really worried about people's opinions; he had a family and gave them all his love. Natalie had to attend a special school and she needed to know she is loved. His daughters loved music just like him and it was a tradition in their house to listen to a song every night and Charlie would tell the girls a story.

The three were inseparable and had a very special relationship, he would bath them, dress them and make sure their schoolwork was done. Janine just came home while Charlie made sure the food was cooked and the girls were sorted, he was running the home.

The girls wanted a dog and Charlie adopted a pit bull. Of all the breeds available, he chose a pit bull. His name was Chester and was only three months old when he joined the family. He taught the girls what responsibility was by giving Chester water and food. He heard many years ago that children that are raised with animals are more stable and was not sure if it was true, but he knew for a fact his girls were becoming responsible and it was a beautiful sight.

Janine, on the other hand always found embarrassing Charlie infront of the girls as entertainment. It was not always a pleasant sight, she used to call him names, and sometimes smacked him, especially when the girls were around. Through all this, his two daughters still love their daddy and treasured him. He had this tradition going with them, he will buy them a party pack every Friday from the aunty at work and they looked forward to this treat. Charlie saw in the movies how fathers would read stories to their daughters and the fun they had. He started it as well. Never had he told his stepfather Anton that he loved him but with his daughters, he made it a rule to tell them every day he loves them. All the things he wanted as a child, or was deprived of, he made sure the girls received it. One day he had a conversation with his daughters.

Charlie: "Natalie and Melony, kom gou hie na Daddy toe?"
Melony: "Yes Daddy, coming," she answers.
Natalie: "Yes old man coming," she giggles. She was the funny one.
Charlie: "You two know I love you right?"
His daughters reply, "Yes, Daddy."
Charlie: "I need to you tell you something."
His daughters reply simultaneously, "What is it Daddy?"
Charlie: "You need to know I love you and you can talk to me about anything, and you should never be afraid to open up to me, I am your dad and I love you."
Melony: "Daddy, why are you and Mommy always fighting?"

Charlie knew the kids were getting big and that they starting to pick up that there are problems.
Charlie: "Uhm you see grown-ups fight from time to time, it's normal," knowing he is lying and that he and Janine has problems, he had to think of something to cover himself.

He could not understand how fast his relationship with Janine has deteriorated in such a short time. They used to be so in love, and he feels like he has disappointed his daughters. He remembers how Anton used to hit his mother and the atmosphere at home was always tense. He promised he would never create that environment for his kids. He and Janine were so in love, by blaming himself, by telling himself he is not trying hard enough.

CHAPTER 17

Muizenberg

It was a hot Saturday morning and the two decided to go to Muizenberg Beach. They took the taxi and did not want to burden Charlie's friends. The taxi drove from Parkwood to Wynberg and from there the two took the train.

On Saturdays, the trains are not that full. However, that is if the trains arrive on time or at all. Charlie had his manga, Pepe T-shirt and Rider slippers on. Sam was also in a manga, Levi T-shirt, Nike slippers and a Karrimor with their food in for the day. The two sat next to each other holding hands, excited to go to the beach.

Sam: "Charlie ons altwee kannie gelyk swem nie, jy kan eerste swem, dan wag ek vir jou." Charlie like a young boy agrees, "Is reg Sam."

The train stops at Retreat and a few people get in the carriage. One of the girls recognises Sam and tells her other friends. Out of the blue, one of the girl's asked, "Waars jou man dan?" Sam looks at her and says, "Is mossie jou besigheid nie."

The train is quiet for a few minutes when one of the other girl's replies, "Is van sleg wil wies." Charlie getting irritated now also chimes in, "Hello, moettie vir julle bis hou nie." Now the girls start attacking Sam, not knowing the real story. It is here where Charlie decided he had enough.

Charlie: "Sy en dai vark is geskei. Hy slat mos vroumense, nou julle cover vir soe 'n gemors daai maak vir julle net soe sleg." He regrets doing this out of anger because the wrong words came out and it is now to late to take back those words. The girls talk amongst each other and one girl send a message to someone on her BBM. The girls just ignored Sam and Charlie after that out burst.

Sam: "Charlie is mense soes die wat niks weet nie en altyd die slegste van almal dink," this followed by tears. Charlie wants to get out at the next station, but Sam tells him not to do it, they will enjoy their day irrespective of what these people said. Sam also remembers who the one girl is. She was one of the girls who use to come to Tony a lot.

Sam: "Het jy vir jou vrinne gesê hoe sleg jy is? Is môs jy wat saam met my man geslaap het." The rest of the train is now watching "Cheaters" for free. This girl does not have a come back.

Sam: "Ek het soe gedink, nou is jou bek stil! By the way jy kan hom maar kry, ons is nou geskei en die is my man hier langs my."

This girl's friends moved away from her as the spotlight is now on her. At the next stop, she and her friends got off, feeling very embarrassed and you could hear them scolding at their friend for embarrassing them.

The other uncles and aunties that's also on their way to Muizenberg applauded Sam and one of the aunties shouts, "Jy't hulle bekke lekka stil gemaak meisie." The train stops at Muizenberg Station, Charlie puts his arm around Sam and says, "Ek's lief vir jou, en ek sal jou nooit lossie," as he kisses her on the cheek and they disembark the train and walk to the beach.

The two newly weds enjoyed themselved at the beach. Charlie even bought Sam an ice-cream at the corner shop that has been there for many years.

Charlie: "As my stief toppie my altyd soe geslat het, dan hardloop ek Muizenberg toe, altyd seker gemaak ek het geld op my virre ice cream."
Sam: "Hoekom het hy jou soe geslaan?"
Charlie: "Ek was nooit sy kind nie, ek is deur hel met hom Sam, but ek dank elke dag die man van Bo ek het jou ontmoet."
Sam: "Ek is oek bly djy is in my lewe Charlie."

They made their way back to the train station and wanted to forget about what happened earlier that day. Charlie promise Sam he will always be there for her and that nothing will ever come between the two of them.

CHAPTER 18

Forgiveness

Charlie and Sam were at Premium Sports Bar, celebrating Liverpool's win against Manchester United and decided to celebrate it with the locals. Charlie was a big Liverpool fan and Sam did not really like soccer, she only did it to support Charlie.

After the match, they went home, and Charlie decided to be romantic and played some nice slow jams. Sam started to glow and something about her seemed different and he had to make sure he kept her happy in all departments. He thinks of the first night he tried to kiss her and how it ended. Now that they are together, he feels, as the man, it is also his responsibility to make sure she is kept happy. You can so easily drift away from your partner and without noticing you can be complete strangers, that is what happened to him and Janine.

Kenny G is playing the saxophone in their room, he bought him a G-string at Edgars in Wynberg, and it was one of those name brand ones. He tells Sam he has a surprise for her, Sam very excited to see this surprise.

Sam: "Het jy alweer van the Silver Bullet tablets gekoep Innie China Town," laughing herself in a state.
Charlie: "Jy issie funny nie Sam," shouting from the toilet.
He enters the bedroom with a red and white G-string on. He got Sam's attention, entertains her while the music is playing, talking with a Russian accent.

Charlie: "Miss Sam I AM UR DANCER FOR RE NIGHT."
Sam laughing as he tries to impress her with his fake accent. He removes the blanket from the bed, pulls Sam to the foot end of the bed. The mood has now change from humorous to a more serious one. He wants to remove her panty and finds it is already off.

Sam: "Ek's een voor vir jou Mr Charles."
Charlie: "Ek sien soe."

He gets ready to let his submarine enter the battle zone; he removes the front part of the G-string. As he gently releases the submarine into the water and feels the warmth of the water. At the same moment, there was a knock on the door.
Sam: "Wie kan dit wies?" She moves her body away from Charlie.
Charlie: "Hulle kan wag Sam, ons maak klaar, en wie te hel visit mense die tyd vannie aand?"

Charlie gets dressed to check who it might be. He's upset and wants to get this over and done so he can continue his submarine adventures. He gives Sam a few minutes to get dressed and opens the door. As he opens the door, he sees a familiar face in front of him with his wife. It is Reggie his brother and his wife Vinolia, wonder what he wants. Still upset that none of them came to the wedding and wondering what they want.

Reggie: "Yes Charlie, hi Sam."
Charlie a bit upset mumbles back, "Yes Reggie, hi Vinolia."
Sam: "Charlie lat jou family in kom, sorry ons huis is nou nie groot nie," trying to be very friendly. Charlie not wanting them there, "Ja, ko ma in."
There is quietness and Sam can also sense Reggie's wife is very full of herself as she looks around to see how the house looks, pulling her jacket tight.
Sam sees the attitude and watches her from an angle.

Reggie: "Dus Derrie"
Charlie: "Jy mean Anton, wat makeer hy."
Vinolia interrupts rudely, "Jou pa, Charles."

Sam looks at her and wants to say something but tells herself it's not her place but definitely next time, no one speaks to her Charlie like that.

Charlie: "Wat van hom?"
Reggie: "Hy lê op sy laaste en wil jou sien."

The memories play back of an abusive stepfather and the pain Charlie felt surfaces instantly as he reminisces of the bad old days.

Charlie: "Ek's sorry om te hoor. Sterkte vir jou wat sy family is," he says.
Reggie: "Hy is in Constantia hospital en wil jou sien."
Charlie: "Is ok Reggie, ek het niks om vir hom te sê nie."
Vinola: "Wat soorte kind is jy?"

Sam couldn't help herself anymore and respond, "As jy Charlie geken het soes die mense wat lief is vir hom sal djy verstaan hy was 'n goeie kind" as she stares at Vionolia, Reggie feels the tension and asks Charlie to consider it.

The couple leaves and Charlie in another mood makes his way to the room as he locks up.
Sam lying next to him and playing with his chest hair.

Sam: "Is jy ok Charlie?"
Charlie: "Hulle het die audacity om vir my te sê ek moet vir hom visit."
Sam: "Charlie jy moet forgive, ek wiet dit wassie jou fout nie, but jy het healing and closure nodig in jou lewe."
Charlie thought about this before and never thought it will happen so soon. The two fell asleep as they lay in each other's arms.

The next morning, they wake up and Charlie is quiet the whole day thinking about visiting Anton. He cannot get to convince himself to go to the hospital.
Later that day he thinks of his mother Mandy and that she asked him to be nice to Anton, he tells Sam he will visit Anton and hear what he has to say.

Charlie: "Sam sal jy saam met my hospitaal toe gat?"
Sam: "Off course Charlie, moet nie worry nie alles gaan ok wees."

What will he talk about, what if Anton wants to bully him one more time? They leave the evening to visit Anton. They get to the hospital and all the other family members are also there. They are shocked to see Charlie there. One uncle asks out of the blue, "Waar kom jy vandaan?" Reggie steps in and said, "Los vir Charlie, julle kan mos nie nou nog vir hom blame vir ou kak nie." There was silence and Reggie took Charlie to his father while Sam waits in the waiting room.
 As Charlie enters the room, he sees a very thin Anton lying there as if he is going to pass away anytime soon.

Reggie: "Derrie, hie is Charlie."
Anton trying to catch his breath looks at Charlie and says, "Hello Charlie," in a deep voice, then trying to catch his breath again.
Charlie not knowing how to answer Anton, remembers Anton telling him not to call him Dad and also never to speak to him. Charlie replies, "Hi."

Reggie wants to leave the room, but his father asks him to stay.

Anton: "Charlie ek moes al lankal vir jou om verskoning gevra het, ek het jou soos 'n hond behandel."

Tears starts rolling from his eyes as he regrets his decision. Charlie confused and also not sure how to respond to Anton.

Charlie: "Is ok, moettie nog worry nie." He made a promise to his mom and plans on still honouring it.

Reggie now also starting to become emotional because he knew how Charlie was treated and the abuse he had endured.

Reggie: "Charlie vergewe vir my ook asseblief."

Charlie: "Ek was nog nooit kwaad vir jou nie Reggie, jy's my baby broertjie."

Charlie: "Anton, jy verstaan nie hoe seer jy my gemaak het nie. Die aande wat ek myself aan die slaap gehuil het. Dit was nie maklik vir my nie maar ek het my ma belowe ek sal nice wees met jou. Ek het jou lankal vergewe al, vir my om aan te beweeg moes ek jou vergewe het."

Anton: "Jammer Charlie, ek het jou baie seer gemaak." He reaches out for Charlie's right hand, holds it in his hand and then kisses it. Charlie had mix emotions, he never expected this to ever happen. Charlie feels a warmness and calmness over comes him as he takes a deep breath. There is an instant relieve, all the sorrow and burdens feel as if it has been lifted amongst the three. Anton ask Reggie to call the rest of the family, as they enter, they see Charlie standing next to Anton holding hands. Anton tells Reggie to tell the family that he has asked Charlie for forgiveness and that Charlie had done nothing wrong and it was him that was jealous.

CHAPTER 19

Inheritance

A few weeks after the passing of Anton, Charlie gets a call from a white man.

Man: "Middag is dit Charlie Daniels?"
Charlie: "Ja wie soek hom?"
Man: "Mnr jy is in die testament van die wyle Anton Fortuin.

Charlie did not expect this and was not sure if he wanted anything from Anton. He calls his brother Reggie and discusses the matter at hand.

Charlie: "Reggie is ekke Charlie, ek dink daar's 'n mistake met Anton se inheritance."
Reggie: "Hoe mean jy Charlie?"
Charlie: "Hulle sê ek het oek geerf."
Reggie: "Is reg Charlie, hy't jou oek in sy will gesit."
Charlie: "But dit wassie nodig nie."
Reggie: "Hy wou dit doen, hy't 'n brief oek met die lawyers vir jou gelôs."

Charlie still very confused speaks to Sam about this.
Charlie: "Samantha, ek moet jou iets vertel!"
Sam: "Wat is dit Charlie?"
Charlie: "Is Anton, hy het my in sy will gesit."
Sam: "Wow, Mr Charles is nou 'n geld gat," as she giggles.
Charlie: "Ek deserve dit nie, hy kan dit vir Reggie gee."
Sam: "Charlie, dus miskien sy way om jou te wys hy is sorry en wie wiet, miskien kan jy my overseas vat. Wink! Wink!"

The next week he arrives at the lawyer's office.
He receives a letter that is addressed,
'To Charlie My Son'. Reggie and Charlie are the only people in the office and waits for the lawyer. Anton had worked at the navy for many years and had retired well.

The lawyer enters and brief the two brothers that the will states everything is 50/50. Anton's estate was worth three million and the lawyer was instructed to sell everything and split the money amongst the two brothers. Charlie still in shock did not even read the letter. The meeting is over, and Charlie heads home to tell Sam what has happened.

Sam: "Charlie jy's mos 'n millionaire nou, wil jy nie met my trou nie?" Knowing that she is teasing him.
Charlie: "Sam ons kan nou onse droom huis koep."
Sam: "Ja, maar dus jou geld Charlie, wat oekal jy decide ek's saam met jou."

A few days later Charlie and Sam made an appointment with an estate agent. Ready to purchase their dream home in Grassy Park in Misrole Avenue. Three months after they moved into their new home Sam discovers a new family member will join them soon. Charlie was very excited and blessed that they are having another family member at almost forty years of age.

Charlie: "Assit 'n girl is noem ons haar Mandy."
Sam: "Ja Charlie en 'n boy noem ons hom Malcolm."
Charlie: "Hoekom Malcolm, Sam?"
Sam: "My pa se naam was Malcolm."
Charlie: "Ek likes die naam."

Charlie and Sam didn't expect to be parents, but it was a blessing. After experiencing what they had, this would be a new chapter in their lives. Charlie always wanted a son and after they killed Chester, he also decided to adopt another pit bull called Max. Starting over is not always bad but it depends on who you starting over with and Sam was the perfect partner to start a new venture with.

Charlie also had enough money to buy a car and decided to settle for a Polo they bought in Tokai. Charlie wanted to drop the car, put on mags and a system but it is here where Sam reminded him of a need and a want, and they do not need that fancy things on the car.
Sam: "Charlie wiet jy dat jou kar gaan nie meer expensive word as jy dit modify nie?"

Charlie: "Ja Sam but dit lyk net kwaai, imagine hoe gat ons twee lyk in daai kar Sam?"
Sam: "Charlie dus jou geld, en die kar lyk fine netsoes dit nou lyk."

Charlie decides that Sam is right, and he needs to manage his money properly. With our economy that is not doing to good it might be a good time to spend money responsibly.

CHAPTER 20

The Letter

Charlie decides one day to read the letter Anton wrote to him and never expected the unexpected. The reason he took so long to read it was because he still had that fear of being abused by Anton even though they made peace the night at the hospital. Charlie was not sure if he should read it or just throw it away. He consults Sam on the matter.

Charlie: "Sam dink jy ek moet die brief van Anton lees?"
Sam: "Ek het gedink jy het dit klaar gelees?"
Charlie: "Noggie."
Sam: "Charlie dus jou decision, but jy sallie kan aan move as jy dit nie gelees hettie."

Charlie not sure and leaves it for later the night when Sam is asleep, he then opens the letter and it reads as follows:

Aan Charlie

As jy die brief lees beteken dit dat ek nie meer op die aarde is nie en dat ek nie kans gekry het om met jou te praat nie. Charlie ek sit hier met trane in my oë en besef dat ek jou en jou ma baie seer gemaak het asgevolg van my insecurities. Na jou ma se dood het ek jou uit gesit waar ek jou pa moes gewees het.

Ek het nooit vir jou ma jammer gevra nie, dus wat aan my gevreet het vir jare. Wat tussen ek en jou ma gebeur het was nie jou fout nie, ek moes jou nooit so getreat het nie. Jy is in my testament en ek weet dit kan nooit reg maak vir wat ek aan jou gedoen het nie.

Charlie ek vra asseblief dat jy my sal vergewe en dat jy agter jou broer sal kyk. Ek was nie die man wat ek moes wees nie. Ek was nie eers by jou troue nie, ek kon nie dit in my hart kry om te kom nie. Ek het jou baie seer gemaak en het nie verdien om jou troue by te woon nie.

Dus ek wat Reggie op gemaak het teen jou, ek het die familie ook teen jou op gemaak. Wat soorte pa was ek? Ek voel so skuldig en soos 'n gemors. Die een wat jou skool boeke weg gesteek het, ek wou hê jy moes druip. Jy het elke keer vir my verkeerd bewys, toe ek die ouer moes wees was jy meer volwasse as ek.

Ek was jaloers op 'n kind wat niks verkeerd aan my gedoen het nie. Charlie ek vra dat jy dit in jou hart vind om my te vergewe. Die geld wat ek jou gelos het sal nooit ooit reg maak waar ek verkeerd gemaak het nie, maar vind dit tog in jou hart om my te vergewe. Ek het nie vir Sam ontmoet nie maar sy is 'n goeie mens kyk mooi na haar. Sy klink soos 'n amzing persoon, kyk asseblief agter haar.

Charlie, ek wil hê jy moet my 'n guns doen, jy hoef nie, maar ek vra jou mooi. Charlie ek wil hê jy moet agter Reggie kyk en sy ouer boeta wees. Ek is nie meer op aarde nie, Reggie is maar baie sag groot gemaak en het nog nie die lewe ervaar soos jy nie. Al die beste vir jou en Sam. Ek hoop ek kry eendag weer die kans om jou te ontmoet sodat ek kan opmaak.

Groete
Anton, Jou Pa

This Chapter is dedidated to our families on the Cape Flats who lost their loved ones in a cruel manner. May God strengthen you and be your guide. We have lost many inncocent lives on the Cape Flats and some of these stories do not even make the headlines.

CHAPTER 21

Familly Matters

One Tuesday morning, Charlie received a call from Aunty Loraine, Janine's mother. Janine never returned home from work and their two daughters are worried about their mother. Charlie told Sam and went to the family house in Cafda by himself. Janine moved back to her mother after the divorce.

Janine's mother said, she left the Saturday already and never came home. Charlie reported the matter at Grassy Park Police Station and let close family and friends know about Janine that was missing. He cannot disappoint his two daughters now. He drove around to the places she was last seen at. With all the women disappearing on the Cape Flats every week, what if Janine is one of them?

Although they are divorced, they have two daughters and he will make sure he finds the mother of his children. He cannot wait for the detective to come from leave to investigate Janine's case and asked his friend to see if he could trace the cellphone as a favour.

While his friend is trying to trace Janine's cell number he fetched his two daughters and dropped them off at his house with Sam and their brother Malcolm.

Charlie received a call from his friend confirming that the phone has been tracked in Lavender Hill. He called two of his buddies to go with him. David and Lance are on standby after Charlie told them what had happened. He picked them up because he cannot go alone.
 What if the guys have guns? Upon arrival at Ashley Court he got out and knocks on a door, waiting for someone to open up. A few minutes later and old lady opens up and ask him what he wants.

He explained to her that he traced Janine's cell phone to her address. The lady closes the door as she tells him there is no phone in her house. He can tell the lady is lying and feels hopeless. David tells him not to force it and rather go to the police station. When they arrive at the police station everyone was on lunch and the detective was still on leave. A young constable notices Charlie and offers his assistance. There is no time for a warrant, what if Janine is in the flat and needs help?

The constable follows the three men back to the flat in Lavender Hill. The constable knocks on the door and the lady opens once again. He told her he has a warrant to search the place.

The woman does not hesitate to hand the phone to the constable, "My kleinkind het dit hier gebring."
Constable: "Mevrou die foon is gesteel en die persoon aan wie die foon behoort is vermis, ek stel voor dat u saam ons werk anders kan u in groot moeilikheid beland. Ek hoop u verstaan die erns van die situasie."
Lady: "Ja Meneer, my kleinkind is 'n Mongrel en hy't die phone hier gebring, sy naam is Gesantjie. Meneer sal hom kry op Retreat se taxi rank."
Constable: "Het jy 'n foto van die Gesantjie?"
Lady: "Ja Meneer ek het, wag netso,
ek kry dit gou vir jou."

The three men left with the constable and head for Retreat Taxi Rank. Charlie needs to find Janine; he just hopes nothing serious has happened to her. When they arrived at the rank, they immediately start asking the people on the rank if they know Gesantjie.

One of the people showed the constable where he is. Gesantjie saw the constable and tries to run but David a previous Western Province runner from Grassy Park High, manages to catch him and made sure he got in a few blows as well. The police officer is interrogating Gesantjie about where he got the phone.

Constable: "Jy waar kry djy die gesteelde phone?"
Gesantjie: "Ek het dit op getel my Larnie."

Constable: "Moettie kak praat nie, ek gaan jou vir die laaste keer vra."
Gesantjie: "Ek het dit by ander tik koppe gekoep my Larnie."

Charlie thinking of his daughters and gets very emotional. He punches Gesantjie that he lands on his back.
Gesantjie: "Djy kan my nie soe slattie, ek ken my regte."
Constable: "As jy my nie nou nie sê waar jy die phone gekry het nie, gee ek jou vir die drie ouens." He uses this scare tactic to get him to spill the beans.

Lance that has observed everything gets really frustrated and tells the constable to give Gesantjie to the three of them. Gesantjie now a bit worried because he knows if the cop gives him to these three guys, they are going to beat him or probably kill him.
Gesantjie: "Ok ek sal praat met jou by die police station en ek wil 'n lawyer hê."

The cop puts him in the police van and drives to the station where one of his senior officers assists him. Charlie is worried about Janine and he hopes that she is ok, wherever she might be. Gesantjie starts talking and tells the officers they hijacked a black Golf Gti 5 with two ladies in it. He described a lady that fits the description of Janine. They took both ladies, the car and drove to a few places with the two of them in the boot. They decided to kill the ladies the Monday morning and buried them somewhere at Strandfontein beach and the car was sold to a chop shop. The cops took Gesantjie with them to go see if what he said was true. They found Janine buried in the clothes she was last seen in. Her hands were tied behind her back and a sock in her mouth. Her friend was buried next to her, both in shallow graves and their faces were covered in dry blood. One of the cops called Charlie over to identify the body. He saw Janine and started crying hysterically.

Charlie asked the cop, "Hoe doen mense die? Djy jou gemôs jy't my kinnes se ma dood gemaak, ek moet jou oek soema vrek maak." David and Lance took their friend one side and tried to comfort him.

Gesantjie now blaming his friends for the murder and gave the names to the cops telling them he was forced to do this and did not have a choice. The young constable also a father told him, "Jy het gewiet wat jy doen, jou vrinne en jy gat sit, ek gaan seker maak. Jy het twee kinders se ma dood gemaak. Julle het die twee vrouens wreed vermoor en miskien is jy oek involve in ander cases, ons sal uitvind Boeta, glo my."

David drives the car to Janine's mom; Charlie was not in a state to drive and sat next to David while Lance sat at the back. When they arrived at Janine's mom's house, Charlie knocks on the door and immediately he starts crying. Aunty Loraine opens up, and upon seeing the tears, she knew Janine was dead and collapsed just there in the lounge. Charlie waits for her to recover and calls a relative to stay with Aunty Loraine.

On their way to his house, he asks David and Lance, "Hoe sê jy vir jou laaties hulle ma is dood? My broer die wêreld is cruel, dai brasse gaan vier jaar kry dan kom hulle weer uit."
Lance: "Charlie my broer, miskien moet jy eers vir Sam sê dan kan jy miskien liewers later of môre met jou dogters praat."
David: "Ek stem saam met Lance my broer, but is up to jou Charlie, ons sal altyd hier wies vir jou my broer."
Charlie immediately called Sam aside while Malcolm is playing with his two sisters under the supervision of his two friends David and Lance.

Sam: "Wat's fout Charlie?"
Charlie: "Dus Janine."
Sam: "Het julle haar gekry?"
Charlie: "In Strandfontein."
Sam: "Wat het sy daar gemaak Charlie."
Charlie: "Sy is dood Sam, hulle het haar en haar vriendin gekidnap en wreed dood gemaak."
Sam: "OMW, wat?"

Sam hugs Charlie and comforts him as he starts to cry again. She thanked him for finding Janine and told him that he is such a good father. She is so proud of him for finding Janine. Sam advised Charlie to wait a few days before he breaks the news to his daughters about their mother's death.

CHAPTER 22

The Funeral

Two things Charlie never imagined he would do was to tell his daughters their mother was brutally murdered and to arrange the funeral. Charlie only had a few days to get everything sorted for Janine's funeral. He had to see Gesantjie one more time. No visitors were allowed but the constable made it possible. Gesantjie was hand cuffed, sitting in a dark room.

Charlie: "Vertel my exactly wat gebeur het daai aand toe julle vir Janine dood gemaak het?"
Gesantjie: "Ek het môs klaar die Boerre vertel."
Gesantjie looks different, his eyes were red, and he seemed possessed or something.
Gesantjie: "Ok as jy wil wiet dan sal ek jou vertel," he smiles. "Ek het eers jou girlfriend gesoen voor sy dood is. My bra het altwee gerape, wat maak hulle dan alleen innie kar sonder enige man?"

Charlie feeling a rage coming over him but he needs to hear the full story so he can get closure on the story.
Charlie: "Ek sien, het dit julle laat voel soes mans?"
Gesantjie: "My bra het hom enjoy met hulle twee!"

Ons het gegaan vir a ride but toe try jou girl mos weg hardloop, ek het haar gevang en hard gemoer met die agterste van my gun."

Her last hours on earth was hell, a previous convicted criminal murdered Janine for no reason.

Charlie: "Hoekom het julle nie net die kar gevat en weg gery nie?"
Gesantjie: "Hoe mean jy dan nou, ons wil môs a good time met hulle gehad het, as hulle vir hulle behave het, sou altwee nog gelewe het." He said it without any remorse. "Plus, daai girl van jou was nogals oulikkies."

Charlie decides to leave, as he gets up, he tells Gesantjie, "Jy bieta sieka maak ons meet mekaar nooit in die afterlife nie, dan kan ons die settle,"
as he walks away.

Sam has been supportive towards Charlie; the couple has really matured over the last few months and their love has grown. Sam tells Charlie his daughters should live with them; it is only right that they move in and also get to know their little brother.

The day of the funeral, Sam tells Charlie that it is ok to cry, at one stage he was married to Janine and they shared a love for each other. Memories replay in Charlie's mind of him and Janine from the first night they met to their wedding day.

The birth of their two daughters, he really loved her and when he married her, she made him forget about his hurtful childhood.

In the church the pastor preached and said, it has become a norm on the Cape Flats for him to bury babies, five year old children, young people who did not see their twenty first birthdays, and women who were raped and killed.

Pastor: "Dit is 'n norm in ons gemeenskap, die wet het sy krag verloor! My broers en susters môre is vir niemand belowe nie, laat ons lewe asof dit die laaste is en reg wees as die Here ons kom haal."

Aunty Loraine, Janine's mom cannot believe she has to say goodbye to her baby. They spoke about going to Sun City as a family for a holiday and they would have gone by aeroplane. Janine was very excited and told her mom she wanted to apologise to Charlie for hurting him, she wanted to move on and be happy again.

The pastor got ready to lower the casket. Charlie touches the casket and makes a promise to Janine, he will take care of their daughters and make sure justice is served. A tear dropped as he said his last goodbyes. Sam was right next to Charlie and put her arm around him as the family walked back to the cars.

Charlie feels very heartbroken all of a sudden, his daughters cried as well and that will break any father but as they drove home, he promised his girls he will take of care of them and that everything will be ok. Charlie was sitting in the dinning room and the telephone rings, it's Aunty Loraine. Sam picks up the phone and calls Charlie.

Sam: "Charlie dus Aunty Loraine vir jou."
Charlie thinking he forgot to do something at the funeral.
Charlie: "Hello Aunty Loraine."
Aunty Loraine: "Hi Charles, ek wil manet dankie sê vir alles my kind."
Charlie: "Is reg Aunty, ek's bly ek kon help."
Aunty Loraine: "Dan is daar nog een iets wat ek vir jou wil sê."

Charlie is wondering, what it can be, maybe she wants to ask if his daughters can live with her.
Aunty Loraine: "Laas week het ek en Janine nog gepraat, sy wou jou gevra het om haar te vergewe Charlie. My kind was regtig jammer oor alles en as haar ma, vra ek dat jy dit in jou hart sal vind om haar te vergewe."
Charlie: "Ek het haar al lankal vergewe, Aunty Loraine."
Aunty Loraine: "Dankie Charlie, jy's 'n goeie mens en bring die girls om na my toe vir 'n visit van tyd tot tyd."
Charlie: "Ek maak so Aunty."

The words of the pastor replays to Charlie "Tomorrow is promised to no one, live as if it is your last day."

CHAPTER 23

Counting Your Blessings

A few months after the funeral, the kids have settled in with their father and Sam. Charlie is very impressed with Sam, she treats his daughters as her own and they share a very special bond. He feels blessed to have a healthy family, especially having a history with an abusive background.

Sam has this idea of giving back to her community and help other women who have been in her situation, but how will she manage? She is a mother of three children now and time is a bit limited. Where Charlie, on the other hand is now thinking of going to church, he remembers his mom Mandy one day said, "A family that prays together, stays together."

However, how do you select a church? As a father, it is his responsibility to make sure he only gives the best to his children and wife Sam. One morning, there is a knock on the door, Sam is still asleep. Charlie gets up and check who is at the door. It was a woman looking for something to eat.

Charlie ask the lady to just hold on, while he gathers tins of food and left-over food from the night before. He also goes to the bedroom to fetch a R50. The woman did not expect any of this, just something to eat.
She started to cry and thanked Charlie for being so kind to her. Charlie felt in his spirit to let the woman in and make her a decent breakfast. Sam also got up to see what Charlie is up to and why he is so busy this morning. The woman's name was Maria. He could see that she was a beautiful woman in her younger days, but he cannot stop wondering, what has gone wrong in her life.

Sam now joins Charlie and Maria. She introduces herself, "Hello Mevrou ek is Sam, sy vrou."
Maria: "Hello Sam nice to meet you, you have a great husband. Please hold onto him."
Sam: "Yes he's chained to me," laughing like always.

Charlie feels that he wants to help this woman and calls Sam one side while Maria is eating her breakfast.

Charlie: "Sam hoe kan ons vir haar help?"
Sam: "Maar ons kennie eintlik vir haar nie, Charles ons kannie almal trust nie, but ek wil oek vir haar graag help, sy klink soos 'n lekker aunty."

Charlie opens his heart and tells the aunty to freshen herself up in their bathroom and Sam will give her something to wear. Maria thanked the couple; she has not been in a bath for weeks.

After almost an hour, Maria comes out of the bathroom, she looks so different now that the dirt has been washed off her face. Somehow, Sam feels this woman has been through some sort of abuse and she starts making conversation.

Sam: "Maria van waar is jy?"
Maria: "My regte naam is Anthea, ek het weg gehardloop van my man. Hy het my abuse en sy vriende het my verkrag."

Charlie listening to the conversation but did not want to interfere, leaves Sam to talk to Maria.

Sam: "My vorige man het my ook geslaan, ek wiet wat jy deurgaan, onthou dus nie JOU fout nie," remembering how she used to blame herself and the low self-esteem she had.

There was just something about Maria, she was different. Charlie asked her, if he can take her to a doctor and he will pay for it and he will purchase a few clothing items for her.

Maria agreed, but Charlie wanted to do this on one condition. She needs to allow him and Sam to help her. This feels so right, and this is how they want to help change other people's lives. While Sam, Charlie and the children are waiting in the reception area of the doctor's surgery, Sam tells Charlie, "Wiet jy hoe het ek gebid dat die Here my 'n sign moet gee hoe ek ander vrouens kan help wat dieselfe problems as my geface het, en hier kom die vrou in onse lewe."

Charlie: "Sam ek stem saam met jou, deur alles wat ek en jy saam deur is, dink ek dus tyd dat ons iets begin waar ons mense kan help.

Maria comes out of the doctor's office after she had a HIV test done. The information is confidential, but Maria decides to tell Sam and Charlie about her status. She has HIV and starts crying. How could her husband that she loved so much do this to her, just because she was unable to conceive. Charlie decides to go after the husband. He is very furious; he wants to teach this guy a lesson he would never forget. Thinking of all the men who has abused the women in his life. That moment, he felt that enough is enough, our justice system has failed our women and children! Sam tells Charlie not to do it.

Sam: "Charlie los dit liewers ons kan haar help om 'n saak te maak, netnou gaan jy tronk toe vir iets en dan sit ek en die kinders sonder jou."
Charlie: "But ek is gatvol van die abuse van mans."

Sam: "Nie al die mans nie Charles, daar is goeie mans soos jy, ek het vir jou gekry en ek dank die Here elke dag vir jou."

Maria agrees to open a case. Sam and Charlie find out that Maria is actually a qualified schoolteacher and her husband a chartered accountant. They discover that abuse comes in every form and shape. When Maria disappeared, her husband opened a case and said she was hijacked and was never found. She has been living on the street for almost six months. If Charlie did not open the door that morning, he would never have known her story.

The couple reaches out to other abuse victims on the Cape Flats and makes sure that they influence people's lives positively as well as raising their beautiful family.

Sam: "Charlie ons was lanklaas kinky."
Charlie: "Ons doen dit gereeld Sam."
Sam: "Ek mean soos daai dag in Cape Point. Ons moet weer dinge op spice Charles."
Charlie: "Djy mean dai."

Everything feels like a dream, this normally only happens in the movies, happy endings does not exist on the Cape Flats, Charlie thinks. Losing his mother due to cancer, his ex-wife to crime and he had to experience abuse from his stepfather.

Sam on the other hand, never got to know her father, like many other children on the Cape Flats. Sam's mother had to raise her and her brothers on her own. Sam was also a victim of abuse, her life at one stage felt it was worth nothing. The couples meeting was a divine appointment.

When the right people meet, they complete each other and yes, it happens on the Cape Flats as well. #jouuncle

Seeing a dead body has become the normal to many Cape Flats Citizens. The pain we endure is unbearable. Most cases, the law cannot be trusted. The perpetrator, if ever caught, does not spend much time in prison. The law is failing us. We must never stop dreaming and chasing after that dream. It is not impossible; you just need to set goals and work towards it daily. Do not stay in a situation that you are not happy in.

Like many people say, "Nothing is worth losing your happiness for." It is ok if people give up on you, but it is not ok if you give up on yourself - #jouuncle

ABOUT THE AUTHOR

Stanley Jacobs is the eldest of six children. He spent the first 7 years of his life, living in Parkwood, Blackbird Avenue. His family then moved to Ottery and after two years, they moved to Grassy Park. Some people referred to Grassy Park as the upper Cape Flats as it was a bit safer.

He is also blessed with a beautiful wife and is a proud father. Besides his love for writing, he is also passionate about music and plays the bass guitar. Stan's journey in the writing industry started a few years ago for a department he used to work at. His colleagues then, enjoyed the content he put together. While being an admin on Cape Flats Stories he decided one day he will write a few stories and to his surprise, people enjoyed his writing and he shared it to a point where he got a request to write weekly. He uses the name **#jouuncle** and his mandate is to make sure the whole world knows about the Cape Flats, mostly the positive side.

Stan says, "I would like to continue writing stories about the Cape Flats, a place that I am very passionate about. I like to refer to myself as a Cape Flats Citizen. My ancestors are originally from Constantia but were forcefully removed by the 1950s Group Act, to the Cape Flats."

Do not let anyone tell you what you can or cannot do, be the best at whatever you decide to do - #jouuncle

Bookings & Orders

Email info@capeflatsstories.co.za

Facebook: @Capeflatsstories

www.ingramcontent.com/pod-product-compliance
Lightning Source LLC
Chambersburg PA
CBHW020009050426
42450CB00005B/380